SHORT CUTS

INTRODUCTIONS TO FILM STUDIES

GERMAN EXPRESSIONIST CINEMA

THE WORLD OF LIGHT AND SHADOW

IAN ROBERTS

WALLFLOWER

LONDON and NEW YORK

A Wallflower Press Book
Published by
Columbia University Press
Publishers Since 1893
New York • Chichester, West Sussex
cup.columbia.edu

Wallflower Press® is a registered trademark of Columbia University Press

Cataloging-in-Publication Data is available from the Library of Congress

ISBN 978-1-905674-60-2 (pbk.)
ISBN 978-0-231-85034-6 (e-book)

Book and cover design: Rob Bowden Design
Cover image: *Nosferatu* (1922), Prana Film

CONTENTS

ACKNOWLEDGEMENTS

As always a great many people have contributed to the development of this book: colleagues and students who were first exposed to much of this material, and friends who have offered useful comments and criticisms at key moments. My gratitude goes to them all. I should like to express particular thanks to Susan Hayward and Will Higbee for their valuable advice and unceasing encouragement throughout the preparation of the manuscript; Paul Cooke likewise deserves my gratitude for planting the seed that eventually grew into this book, and for reading some of the early chapters. Thanks too to my family – Kate, Emily and Tom – for their constant support and love, and for always keeping my feet on the ground ('you're not watching *another* old film, are you daddy?').

Finally to my mother, who never stopped believing in me, and who died before this book was completed.

INTRODUCTION: IMMANENCE, IMAGINATION AND IMMORTALITY

Of all the movements to emerge during the first century of world cinema, few can have been as readily identified with a certain 'look' as the silent, expressionist films which were produced during the ill-fated years of Germany's first attempt at democratic government, the Weimar Republic. For many observers, the stark images of such iconic films as *Das Cabinet des Dr. Caligari* (*The Cabinet of Dr Caligari*, 1920), or *Metropolis* (1927) have come to represent not just an era or a country, but the very essence of the early film industry. These films, and many others produced in the period between the end of World War One in 1918 and the advent of sound in German film in 1930, represent an urge to establish the young medium as equal to the other arts, and were filmed by men and women who believed passionately in the potential of film and thus constantly strove to extend the new medium's technical and narrative possibilities. One of the ways that they sought to achieve this goal was to turn to Expressionism – an artistic movement which had flourished in Germany in the first years of the twentieth century, but which was already losing its vitality and influence by the end of World War One – to lend their films both a certain air of respectability, on a par with the vibrant theatrical scene of the day, but also to set them firmly apart from other national cinemas in Europe and across the Atlantic in Hollywood, all the better to exploit what was already becoming a highly-competitive market. For a few more years, the appropriation of Expressionism in Weimar-era films not only gave them a 'unique selling point' as we might say today, but it also extended the lifespan of the movement and created some of its most enduring images.

In this study I intend to introduce the reader to a number of the prime figures and most influential films of the period known variously as Weimar film or 'expressionist cinema'.[1] The book will outline the principal artistic influences upon these films – not least Expressionism itself – as well as seeking to offer background information on the political and social factors which likewise had an effect upon the nature and content of the films in question. Finally I will offer an analysis of a range of films drawn chronologically from the period, each the product of a different director. To a certain extent any one chapter can be read in its own right: each will offer a brief biography of the director in question and outline their influence on both the domestic and international film industry of the day. In each chapter, too, I place the film in question within its broader generic, historic or thematic context, thus demonstrating how a film both reflected ongoing developments in industry and society, and (in many cases) went on to establish a benchmark against which subsequent films have been measured. In this way I hope to demonstrate how the films selected here illustrate the fluctuating fortunes of the ill-fated Republic in the years before the collapse of democracy and the rise of Hitler's Nazi Party.

Despite mixed fortunes in terms of preservation and availability, the best-known films of the Weimar period have enjoyed renewed popularity in recent years, in part because many have become appropriated as icons within our postmodern age. The cityscape of Lang's *Metropolis*, to focus on just one film, is the acknowledged influence for Ridley Scott's seminal science fiction film *Blade Runner* (1982), while pop videos by Madonna, Queen, Pink Floyd and others have popularised the image of the robot-Maria and the shuffling, downcast workers. Interest in the films of this period has steadily grown: the advent of video and DVD transfers of these films has exposed them to a far broader audience than ever before, earning them due recognition as treasures of a glorious age in film history.

The legacy of World War One and the illusion of normality

Any study of film in the modern era would be hard put to ignore the impact of the terrorist attack on the World Trade Center in New York and the Pentagon in Washington in 2001. The term '9/11' quickly found a resonance within global culture, and from a film perspective, no contemporary cinema-goer in the world could fail to associate a shot of the Twin Towers (or other, essentially unrelated images of towers against a cityscape), with the emotions of horror, or relate them to the subsequent 'war on terror'.[2] In a similar manner, we must view those German films produced between 1918 and 1930 as being fundamentally overshadowed by both World War One and the political debacle of the troubled Weimar democracy.

Thus Weimar films can be better understood when viewed with at least a basic knowledge of the social and political events of their day. Many critics and commentators, for example, fail to consider the realities of World War One, and the harsh conditions endured by the German population between 1917 and 1919, to determine the extent to which these hardships might have informed Weimar cinema, at least in the early 1920s. As we shall see in subsequent chapters, a range of factors may well have influenced a given film: the Spanish influenza pandemic which informs the imagery in F. W. Murnau's *Nosferatu: eine Symphonie des Grauens* (*Nosferatu: a Symphony of Horror*, 1922), for example, or the fact that G. W. Pabst's revolutionary tale *Die Liebe der Jeanne Ney* (*The Love of Jeanne Ney*, 1927) was only given the go ahead by producers who wished to capitalise on the success of Sergei Eisenstein's *Bronenosets Potyomkin* (*Battleship Potemkin*, 1926). Finally, as a reflection of the international nature of cinema even in this early period, it should be recognised that German audiences were just as likely to have watched, say, Douglas Fairbanks in *The Thief of Baghdad* (Raoul Walsh) in 1924 as they were to have marvelled at the performance of Emil Jannings in F. W. Murnau's *Der letzte Mann* (*The Last Laugh*, 1925).

It is the surreal nature of Weimar Germany's existence, then, where periods of rampant inflation, mass unemployment and political rivalry were marked by strikes, street fighting and armed revolt, that adds a fascinating backdrop to the study of the films produced against the backdrop of these tumultuous events. In a sense, Weimar society created the ideal breeding-ground for an art form based fundamentally upon the *illusion* of reality. Cinema is, after-all, primarily a medium of escapism, where reality is put on hold for an hour or two as the viewer sits in a darkened room and consumes the images projected onto the screen. Thus the consumer of the Weimar film – both the cinemagoer in 1920s Germany and we ourselves nearly a hundred years later – succumbs to this cinema of attraction, becoming the realiser of his or her own fantasy world. This must have been particularly important to German viewers in the turbulent postwar years. It can be no surprise that the adventure film was one of the most popular genres in the first years of the Weimar Republic, transporting the viewer to exotic locales which bore little or no resemblance to the world in which they lived. Likewise, historical dramas and, to a certain extent, science fiction, provided what were (on the surface at least) alternatives to the drudgery of daily life. Vicarious thrills could be gained by watching crime series or the filmic versions of the great German *Kammerspiel* (chamber play), where lords and ladies lived cheek-by-jowl with commoners, and the audience was privy to both worlds. Siegfried Kracauer, while he was still living in Berlin, was particularly fascinated by this 'calico world' (see 1995b) as he called it, a world of great imagination and industry, but one where all parties (both the film producers and consumers), willingly accepted the deception which was begun almost as soon as the first sets were constructed.[3]

Why study Weimar films?

So why study Weimar film at all? Thomas Elsaesser identifies an inherent contradiction at the heart of Weimar cinema, which goes a long way towards explaining our preoccupation with the films of this complex and fascinating era:

> What has become abundantly clear is that the cinema permeated Weimar society as a very contradictory cultural force, at once part of oppositional Modernist avant-gardes and in the forefront of capitalism's own modernising tendencies (as technology, industry and fashion) and for this very reason, invested with the hopes of revolutionary changes while being susceptible to being used as the instrument for their containment (in the form of specular seduction, nostalgia, propaganda). (2000a: 151)

Thus film becomes both a commercial product of Modernism, forcing the pace of change both through technological advances in production and in the images which are produced, whilst at the same time acting as a reactionary tool which appears to hinder development in a society gripped by a debate – at times violent – over the direction in which it should be heading.

   Although there are many reasons why we might choose to study these films, then, the answer perhaps lies in the fact that the expressionist 'look', a style which was devised collectively by the directors, set designers, lighting technicians and camera operators (not to mention the financiers, producers and distributors), came to be connoted with the era out of which it sprang. Although the exact definition of the term is now hotly debated,[4] filmic Expressionism first came to be associated with a handful of films which proved relatively successful at home and abroad and was then applied to virtually all films produced in Germany for the best part of a decade and more, as German films became valuable cultural and financial commodities in an increasingly commercialised world. The dream world of Expressionism, artificial worlds of light and shadow captured on celluloid, created a unique approach to *mise-en-scène* which enabled the German cinema industry to challenge, albeit briefly, the growing dominance of Hollywood.

The German directors, thanks to the influence of various literary and artistic movements, set out from the start to saturate their films with images of such visual abundance that they sit on the border between reality and fantasy, creating oneiric visions of great richness. Paul Wegener, one of the first to recognise the unique potential of film to transcend this border in visual terms, wrote as early as 1913:

> Everything depends on the image ... where the fantastic world of the past meets the world of today. I realised that photographic technique was going to determine the destiny of the cinema. Light and darkness in the cinema play the same role as rhythm and cadence in music. (Quoted in Eisner 1969: 40)

Thus the manipulation of the image, far exceeding Max Skladanowsky's or the Lumière brothers' early efforts to record day-to-day details with their pioneering cameras, becomes the overriding goal of the cinema of the Weimar years. Film, through its images, would explore concepts of reality and identity (of which national identity is but one part); it would reanimate the past, and notions of history, myth and legend; it would articulate ancient, atavistic fears; it would cast a spotlight upon the present; and only then might it dare, finally, to posit some notions of the future.

Kracauer boldly stated that 'films are the mirror of the prevailing society', describing the images on screen as coded references to the soul of a society which 'provide unmediated access to the fundamental state of things' (in Levin 1995: 291, 75). A study of the images reveals to us a great deal about the early film industry and also about the society which produces them. There is a transcendent quality to the black-and-white figures who move before us, captured on ephemeral film stock, which enhances the poignant romance of studying these films. To see them projected gives the actors, now dead, an immanence which attracts even as it renders them immortal. This is particularly the case in Weimar films, since we are equally fascinated by the expressionist *mise-en-scène* of the images we see.[5]

Kristin Thompson offers a definition of expressionist film as 'a stylistic term', which she sees as

> applying to a general attempt to minimise the differences among the four aspects of *mise-en-scène*: lighting, costume, figure dispo-sition and behaviour, and setting. The expressionist film makes, as much as possible, a single visual material of these aspects; the result is an emphasis on overall composition. (Quoted in Elsaesser 2000a: 26)

It is perhaps this 'emphasis on overall composition' which sets the expres-sionist film apart. In the first instance, each of the films selected in this book contains one or several of these elements but all achieve the compositional emphasis identified by Thompson above. Naturally these four elements of *mise-en-scène* are present in any number of films from this period, and other eras and cultures of film production, but it is the *blend* of these ele-ments which turns the best examples of expressionist film into what French critic François Berge described as 'marvellously balanced painting[s] of light and shadow' (quoted in Bordwell & Thompson 2001: 407).[6]

Weimar film: chaos or consistency?

Despite the chaotic conditions prevailing in German society through the 1920s, and despite a huge range of themes and subject matter treated by the various filmmakers, Weimar films nonetheless exhibit a number of commonalities which make them instantly recognisable as representa-tions of the Republic's cultural life. Furthermore, these commonalities set them apart from the products of any other national cinema, either of their day or since. This is, no doubt, the primary reason behind the widespread use of the term 'Expressionism' or 'expressionist cinema' to delineate the movement from others in Germany and elsewhere. As will become evident, Expressionism was certainly a significant influence on the films produced in Germany in the years after 1918 but it was by no means the only influence, and its imprint is less easy to discern in the case of films from the middle, relatively affluent period of Weimar. Yet, as we shall see, traces of Expressionism in the form of various signature visuals and a number of thematic concerns linger, even to the end of the period in question. Each of the films examined in this study (and many others besides), display many or most of these elements to a certain extent:

- a remarkable level of collaboration due in no small measure to the Weimar practice of the 'director-unit', whereby each film is unthinkable without acknowledging the role of the scriptwriter, set designer, lighting technician and cameraman (even if we then accept the guiding role of the director as the ultimate influence in each film).

- a desire to combine popular appeal (i.e. box-office success) with an artistic sensibility. This often manifests itself in a desire to present a unique style or a grand production which is in some way unique, apart from artistic predecessors and contemporaries.

- a sense that German film could act as an ambassador for the country at a time when, in the early years of the Republic in particular, German products were shunned (or even banned) elsewhere in the world. Clearly the search for a unique style helped in this area.

- a 'look' which resulted in some of the most carefully-fabricated *mise-en-scène* in the history of cinema, whereby virtually every aspect of a film's shooting was studio-bound and thus carefully controlled. Thus the use of *chiaroscuro* lighting can be discerned in films made well into the 1930s, and is preserved in the Hollywood *noir* thriller of the 1950s by those personnel who chose to emigrate to the USA (*mise-en-scène* and *chiaroscuro* will be examined in more detail in chapter 2).

Moreover, these signature elements are then further interpreted through a number of themes which seem to reflect specific concerns dominating public life at various points in the Republic's existence:

- a sense of threat, to individuals, couples and society at large, which either emanated from within society itself, such as the asylum director in *The Cabinet of Dr Caligari* (see chapter 2), or from external monsters like the vampire Orlok in *Nosferatu* (chapter 3). In fact, this sense of threat, and the horror which accompanies it, is possibly the single most consistent element throughout the films made during the Weimar Republic.

- a desire to appropriate Germany's (supposedly) less vexed past (as in Lang's *Die Nibelungen*) in order to forget the privation and humiliation of the War, and to provide a template for the present (chapter 4).

- a depiction of a dystopian future (as in *Metropolis*) which acts as a warning about present circumstances and conditions (also chapter 4).

- a growing tendency, especially in the later years of Weimar, to focus on rather more realistic depictions of society, examining phenomena which are perceived to be threatening stability, such as the role of the sexually-liberated woman in an age of rapidly-evolving morality (for example, in G. W. Pabst's *Die Büchse der Pandora*, (*Pandora's Box*, 1928), or the tensions created by the modern, urban space which dehumanises the individual (in Joe May's *Asphalt*, 1929), dealt with in chapters 5 and 6 respectively).

- a preoccupation with notions of dream and reality, madness and sanity, and blindness and vision which all seem to be subsumed into a concept of ineluctable destiny for both the individual and the society.

- above all, a desire to show the world in a fantasy light, a liminal space where dreams, imagination and desire may briefly be reconciled with harsh realities.

Thus, even as Weimar cinema presented viewers with the means to escape reality, in actual fact audiences found themselves confronted with a thinly-disguised representation of their quotidian lives which reflected all-too accurately the major concerns of the day.

Naturally there have been some artificial limits placed upon this book in order to maintain its function as an introduction to the films of the period. I have chosen, for instance, to limit the period of 'Weimar film' to the years 1919 – the founding of the Republic – to 1929/1930 (when the advent of sound brought the period of Weimar film to an end, even if the Republic struggled on for a few years more).[7] Furthermore, I have attempted to examine at least one film by each of the directors most commonly regarded as having made the greatest contribution to German expressionist film: Fritz Lang, F. W. Murnau, G. W. Pabst, Robert Wiene, Joe May. Even here choices have been made which will undoubtedly prove contentious; there is no separate chapter on Ernst Lubitsch, for instance, (although a number of his films are discussed) and I have only referred in passing to influential films by the likes of E. A. Dupont, Paul Leni and Paul Wegener. Nor have I examined in detail the *Kammerspielfilm* (chamber play film), the Weimar war film, or the *Bergfilm* (mountain film), even though these are popular genres from this period. Finally, I have (with one notable exception) limited myself to a single case study for each director studied: in the case of Fritz Lang, I stretch that limitation by considering *Die Nibelungen* and *Metropolis* as two sides of the same thematic coin.

Ultimately it is testimony to the visionary genius of the men and women involved in the Weimar film industry that a book such as this struggles to limit itself to a handful of directors and examples of their best films. No matter where we turn, films can be identified which could easily be the subject of further examination. This present study sets out to do no more than introduce the reader to the rich vein of films which may be found in what has come to be known as 'German expressionist cinema'. By presenting some films which are firmly part of an established canon of 'German Expressionism', as well as others which transcend that definition (even if they still display expressionist traces) it is hoped that the student, the film historian and the enthusiastic cineaste alike will find inspiration and reason to explore further the phenomenon of Weimar film.

1   ORIGINS: EXPRESSIONISM AND WEIMAR FILM

So much emphasis has been placed upon Expressionism in German film that it seems at times as if the phenomenon emerged from an industry which had hitherto offered little of quality or interest. Nothing could be further from the truth: like all the major European nations, Germany already had a well-established filmmaking industry by the outbreak of World War One. Single-reel features had given way to two-reel then three-reel melodramas and thrillers, while exhibitions in travelling fairs were gradually superseded by permanent cinemas, as interest in the new phenomenon grew. Similarly, although it is apparent to most students of the period that the cinematic manifestation of Expressionism had its roots in a literary and artistic movement of the same name, the emergence of that movement, and its eventual appropriation by the cinema, is frequently misunderstood. Moreover, it must be remembered that Expressionism was, to all intents and purposes, dead as an artistic movement by the time Robert Wiene's *The Cabinet of Dr Caligari* (which shall be examined in detail in the next chapter) burst onto the world scene in 1920, heralding the advent of expressionist cinema.

The impact of Expressionism on the cinema of the Weimar Republic cannot be underestimated. The use of artificial light and shadows, the atmosphere of unease, exaggerated acting styles, themes of psychological expression and a pervading sense of horror and the supernatural, can all can be traced back to Expressionism in its literary, artistic or theatrical manifestations. Yet, although they are relatively easy to identify on the screen, their precise origins can be difficult to trace.

This is because cinematic Expressionism, like any artistic movement, borrowed many of the elements which make up its 'look' from a wide range of literary, artistic and filmic predecessors. In the distinctive visual style of the films of Lang, Murnau, Wiene and others there can be traced elements of expressionist theatre, Romantic painting, *Jugendstil* and so on (see Eisner 1969); likewise the scripts of Thea von Harbou and Carl Mayer (to name just two of the most prolific scriptwriters from this period) borrowed heavily from the Gothic Horror novel, Classicism, Futurism, folklore, fairy tales and a great many other sources.

Max Skladanowsky and the origins of the German film industry

Although the French brothers Auguste and Louis Lumière are widely celebrated as the inventors of cinema, the pioneering work of German Max Skladanowsky is much less well known. At around the same time as the Lumière brothers, Skladanowsky was using his own 'Bioscop' system to record, and project, 'living photographs' of scenes in and around Berlin (see Jacobsen *et al.* 1993: 14). He quickly graduated to short narrative pieces, and presented these to a fee-paying public in the Berlin Wintergarten on 1 November 1895, several weeks before the Lumière brothers demonstrated their 'cinématographe' to Parisian society.[1] Although film as a new art form struggled to establish itself outside of travelling showgrounds and temporary cinemas, it gradually gained ground as an entertainment form in the first years of the twentieth century, with increasingly lengthy feature films which displayed ever more sophisticated narrative and technical techniques.[2] The 'Kientopp' or 'Kintopp', which came to be known popularly as 'Kino' (cinema), had well and truly arrived in Germany as a form of mass entertainment.

The early sociologist Emilie Altenloh, who investigated the nature of German cinema in the years before World War One, noted the essentially escapist quality of popular films. She suggested that the medium's inherent sensationalism made it ideally suited as a form of entertainment for the working and lower-middle classes, who had neither the time, the money nor the inclination to appreciate the theatre or other fine arts:

> It is not only the fast-paced, overwhelming form of cinema (which is indeed its very element) that so completely satisfies the needs of a broad mass of people: the *content* of cinematic representations

11

also does this. The fact that erotic films and films about criminals attract such large audiences is utterly explicable: surely these films are the only ones that can strike a chord among the mass of people whose intellectual life is often in deep slumber and who have nothing in common with [one] another, at least as far as more elevated matters are concerned. (2001: 258)

Altenloh did accept that such films might be the product of 'extraordinary artistic achievements' (ibid.: 258), but concluded that film was unlikely ever to gain broad approval.[3] The Austrian novelist and playwright Hugo von Hofmannsthal agreed, claiming that 'all the working people are looking for in the movie theater is a substitute for dreams' (2004: 53). Yet with hindsight we can acknowledge that this oneiric quality, the ability of film to transport the viewer to a world of dreams, is precisely why cinema went on to confound its critics, and why the films of the Weimar period contribute to our understanding of the process whereby cinema was transformed from a vaudeville sideshow for the masses to a global entertainment industry and a major art form in its own right. Certainly the German wartime authorities recognised the potential of the medium to entertain and to mobilise the masses, choosing to nationalise the entire industry in 1917 as the 'Bild- und Filmamt' (BUFA, Office for Picture and Film) (see Kreimeier 1999: 21).[4]

Those who had been involved in the founding period of the industry itself soon recognised the medium's potential to release those dreams and thereby to attain the status of art. Surely, they reasoned, film can be both successful, appealing to the masses at one level, whilst also aspiring to the status of an art form. In Germany, once the war was over, this urge to acquire legitimacy for the still young (and re-privatised) medium was almost as great an imperative as was the need to make capital. Erich Pommer, who deserves much of the credit for the inexorable rise of the German film in the 1920s, soon noted cinema's potential to equal, if not eclipse, its predecessors and rivals, in the world of art and entertainment simultaneously. With remarkable prescience, he suggested in 1922 that a number of films would transcend their own era and enter a filmic pantheon, destined to endure for years to come like the great paintings or works of literature: 'I am absolutely convinced that a body of classics will gradually emerge from the mass of films, which will not be overshadowed in their later impact by the classics of the theatre' (quoted in Dalichow & Geiss 1994: 28).

Romanticism: precursor to Expressionism

Cinematic Expressionism, with its emphasis on the contrasts between light and darkness, and a preoccupation with the inner machinations of the psyche, can demonstrate an excellent artistic pedigree. The uniquely-German approach to the European artistic movement known as Romanticism provided the foundations for the first flush of Expressionism in the early years of the twentieth century. In the late-eighteenth century, *Dichter* (the German term connotes both writer and poet) such as Friedrich Schiller and Johann Wolfgang von Goethe, marvelled at nature and ruminated on the individual's relationship with it and with God. By the first half of the nineteenth century, others were becoming more animated by the sense of mysticism which emanated from wild landscapes and ruined castles and abbeys. They saw the rational world of daylight and logic as one side of a natural relationship which placed insanity, horror and fear of the night on the other side. The popular horror tales of E. T. A. Hoffmann in particular drew upon a sensibility of what the Germans called the *unheimlich*, the weird or uncanny, referring to an ill-defined sense of subconscious horror, latent spirits and repressed emotions. This finds visual echoes in the style of the Romantic painters in Germany, most notably Caspar David Friedrich, whose studies of forlorn characters in vast, beautiful but uncaring landscapes touched a nerve with a society which had always displayed a fascination with the natural world. Tales of night-time horrors, wild landscapes and storm-tossed seas, isolated ruins and yet more isolated individuals lost within these landscapes all seem to have inspired the Weimar directors, notably the sea and landscapes which reflect the psychological state of many of F. W. Murnau's characters, for instance (see chapter 3).

The emergence of Expressionism

The roots of Expressionism were to be found in the *fauves* of the French art scene and the German 'secessionist' groups, which were seeking to break with established traditions of artistic representation within their national schools. In *fin de siècle* Vienna, for instance, the *Jugendstil* art nouveau movement (associated today with Gustav Klimt in particular) quickly spread via Bavaria to artistic centres throughout Germany. Like the British Arts and Crafts movement, the aim of the Secessionists was to produce high-quality art which combined the best of medieval handicrafts and a purity of artistic expression with a sensibility which would appeal to the masses in a world of (as they saw it) soulless, industrialised production.

In Germany, secessionist groups sprang up in several areas, including Munich, Berlin, Stuttgart and Dresden. In Munich, the *Blaue Reiter* (Blue Rider) group, founded by Franz Marc, Gabriele Münter and Wassily Kandinsky in 1911 displayed its trademark image of brightly and unrealistically coloured paintings of animals and landscapes – a kind of hyperreality which finds echoes in the expressionist films of the Weimar Republic. In Dresden, the *Brücke* (Bridge) group coalesced out of a number of artistic journals and coffee-house groupings. Here artists such as Ernst Ludwig Kirchner and Karl Schmidt-Rottluff produced stark images of city life, emphasising the dehumanised individual. The German secessionists celebrated life in a riot of colour, abstract shapes and even cubist interpretations: picking up where the German Romantics had left off, they too felt that their vocation was somehow to fuse the visible world with the invisible. As Franz Marc declared, 'art is nothing but the expression of our dream; the more we surrender to it, the closer we get to the inner truth of things' (quoted in Dube 1996: 126).

Gradually these strands fused into German Expressionism. The term was current in Germany by around 1910, when an exhibition in Berlin noted the term in its catalogue. Expressionism quickly spread to every area of artistic endeavour: the theatre of Georg Kaiser, Carl Sternheim and Ernst Toller, the poetry of Gottfried Benn and Georg Heym, and even the atonal symphonies of composer Arnold Schönberg, to cite just a handful of examples.

In fact it is a thankless task to attempt to sum up Expressionism, since it was always a broad, ill-defined movement. 'What is Expressionism?' asks Paul Raabe:

> The term has been exhausted of all meaning by the strife of the historians and ideologues. Once the phenomena of the movement have been more closely examined it is no longer possible to assume any unity of style. (1974: 12).

Once all the disparate elements have been stripped away, for Raabe at least the formula is in fact quite simple: 'Expressionism was atmosphere, movement, vitality' (ibid.).

Above all else, Expressionism in all its manifestations shared a common sense of optimism, albeit one tinged by a morbid anticipation of disaster which would bring about critical change. There was a shared belief that its advocates were helping the world (or at least Europe) to shake off the old established order, one which had prevailed largely unchanged since medieval times. Some awaited the time of *Dämmerung* (literally 'dusk'), elaborated by the neo-Romantic, apocalyptic notions of Richard Wagner's late-nineteenth century *Ring* cycle, where the Ride of the Valkyries is inescapably followed by the *Götterdämmerung* (Twilight of the Gods). The Expressionists thus felt that a radical transformation of European society was imminent, indeed long overdue. In language which seems presciently to anticipate the outbreak of war, Franz Marc declared in the almanac of the Blue Rider group in 1912:

> In our epoch of the great struggle for a new art we 'wilds' [echoing the French term *fauves*], who are without organisation, are fighting against an old, organised power. The struggle appears unequal; but in spiritual matters numbers are never victorious, rather the strength of the ideas. The feared weapons of the 'wilds' are their *new thoughts*: they kill better than steel and can break that which was held to be unbreakable. (1982: 27)

Moreover, the Expressionists' anti-industrialist, anti-bourgeois aspirations were geared towards hastening that change. Some of the more radical were openly modernist, shrugging off the widespread criticisms of the movement's ideals and accepting even the perils of industrialisation in the hope that this too was a means to an end. As Kasimir Edschmid recollected: 'It was a magical time, but we didn't really know why ... The Expressionists were quite naturally shot at from all sides, partly with automatic pistols, partly with laurel wreaths' (1961: 11).

World War One and the death of Expressionism

Against this background, then, it is perhaps easy to see why the majority of expressionists welcomed the advent of World War One. This was to be the cataclysmic event which would bring about the societal transformation they so eagerly anticipated. In contrast to the brightly coloured conflicts of previous centuries, as nations were carved out of the soil, this was to be a war of metamorphosis. With its emphasis on dull uniforms, mechanised transportation and industrial-scale warfare (even those most modern of warfaring machines, the aircraft and the tank), nothing would ever be the same again. It was, literally, to be the war to end all wars. With hindsight it is all too easy to recognise the folly of their optimism, but at the time this attitude was widespread both within German society and throughout the rest of Europe. When war finally came in 1914, the reality of industrialised warfare, the scale of the slaughter, came as a terrible shock. More pertinent still is that a number of the German expressionists, having welcomed the onset of war, had volunteered enthusiastically to participate in this communal act of renewal. As a consequence, many returned from their front line experience suffering from various manifestations of shell shock and mental illness, while a few paid the ultimate price and never came home. Indeed, Franz Marc tragically disproved his own assertion that thoughts 'kill better than steel', when he was killed by a shell splinter on 4 March 1916, during the Battle of Verdun.

The war succeeded in killing the impetus of the movement too: those who returned from the front, and those who had watched the suffering at home of soldier and civilian alike (the Allied blockade of German ports had resulted in terrible privation), almost instinctively turned their backs on an approach to art and life which had been inherently optimistic. The Russian Revolution of 1917, too, had shown that others in Europe had waited long enough for the promised transformation of society into a utopia and had taken matters into their own hands. In postwar Germany, as Allied reparations and occupation took their toll,[5] as different factions struggled on the streets to gain control of a shattered society, artists of all persuasions began to shift their style. Although some might still be termed expressionist, the new starkness of the paintings by the likes of Otto Dix and George Grosz, and the literature of Alfred Döblin, heralded a new era – and a more socially-committed form of art – which came to be known as *Neue Sachlichkeit*, or New Objectivity.[6]

Expressionism in cinema

Thus, by the time that Expressionism was making its presence felt in the cinema it was already a waning influence in other spheres of creativity. A combination of war-weariness and cynicism over the future of Germany, which had brought about the rejection of Expressionism elsewhere, ironically seemed to help the situation with respect to the cinema. Expressionist theatre, for instance, was effectively finished before 1920, while many of the early figures of cinematic Expressionism had their origins in pre-1918 theatre, including the director F. W. Murnau and the actors Conrad Veidt and Emil Jannings. Whilst the Scandinavian cinema had achieved real critical acclaim in the years before the war, with films which quite clearly draw on expressionist elements (notably the *chiaroscuro* play of light and shadow), and thus predates its use by Weimar directors, it was the German cinema industry of the postwar era which gains the label of Expressionism (see Salt 1979).

So it was left to the filmmakers to pick up the torch of Expressionism for just a few short years. It seems as if German cinema and Expressionism found each other at a particularly opportune moment: using the distinctive style of the pre-war expressionists, Weimar's directors could portray the horrors abroad in the world which threatened to oppress and overwhelm the weary individual; depictions of the individual ground down by the twin beasts of capitalism and industrialisation; and explorations of the human psyche and its extreme states. Occasionally, in an echo of the pioneers' optimistic aspirations perhaps, there were even groundbreaking critical examinations of the fundamental nature of society and its relationships: social injustice and the issue of gender equality; a study of the impact of wealth and poverty; pacifism and the perils of extreme nationalism. Of course, the cinema was by its very nature a commercial enterprise, so there is also the question of its motives in embracing a visual style which set apart the products of Germany's Weimar film industry at a time when little else produced in the country was welcome overseas. The unique *mise-en-scène* of these films might even have emerged as no more than a cynical marketing ploy. At one point in Fritz Lang's 1922 thriller *Dr Mabuse der Spieler* (*Dr Mabuse, the Gambler*) the machiavellian master-criminal dismisses out of hand a guest's reference to Expressionism as a sign of Weimar's *Zeitgeist*, seeing in it instead merely a fad, a different form of commercial exploitation: 'Expressionism?' he asks contemptuously, 'It's just a game. Everything is a game nowadays.'

Then again, perhaps the painted strips of light and the use of an exaggerated acting style constituted no more than a response to the acute shortages in power and materials which prevailed in the earliest days of the Weimar Republic. Even when the situation improved in the middle years of the Republic there are plenty of anecdotes revealing just how primitive conditions often were on the set of a Berlin film, certainly in comparison to those which were already the norm in Hollywood. Yet it seems just as likely that the men and women working in the industry, the directors and scriptwriters, the camera operators and set designers working on the films which emerged immediately after the war had simply been touched by Expressionism. They wished to apply their enthusiasm for the movement's ideals to a medium which was seeking to establish itself and to break away from its early reputation as a cheap fairground thrill, inferior to all the other arts, not least its close cousin, the theatre.

Champions of Expressionism: establishing a reputation in film studies

Much of the iconography of the expressionist film, and virtually our entire understanding of Weimar cinema in the first decades after the Second World War, was shaped by two key texts in particular: Siegfried Kracauer's 1947 study *From Caligari to Hitler* and Lotte Eisner's 1952 work *The Haunted Screen*. Kracauer and Eisner were both working as critics and essayists in Berlin in the 1920s but were forced to flee from the Nazis in the 1930s and saw out the war in exile – Kracauer in the USA, Eisner in France. They then subsequently produced critical commentaries of the films they had watched and reviewed in Germany from the unique, and perhaps distorted, perspective of their exile. Their critiques contained a mix of nostalgia and resentment, exacerbated by their dismay over the ruinous legacy of Adolf Hitler for their homeland. In more recent years the work of the film historian Thomas Elsaesser, most notably his study *Weimar Cinema and After: Germany's Historical Imaginary* (2000a), has sought to take advantage of modern film studies techniques, building on the pioneering work of the two luminaries Kracauer and Eisner to offer a more rounded view of the period in question.

Siegfried Kracauer's *From Caligari to Hitler* has been a standard text for students of Weimar film for half a century now. But Kracauer produced his work with a clear agenda: 'This book is not concerned with German films merely for their own sake; rather, it aims at increasing our knowledge of pre-Hitler Germany in a specific way' (1947: ii). Kracauer took film as but one symptom of a German malaise, a longing for a strong leader which had manifested itself in support for Adolf Hitler and National Socialism. The study of films is then one way to understand that malaise: 'In general, it will be seen that the technique, the story content, and the evolution of the films of a nation are fully understandable only in relation to the actual psychological pattern of this nation' (1947: 5). As such Kracauer neglects certain excellent films and offers rather too much on others. It is now clear that his agenda, enshrined within the full title of his work, inadvertently served to colour his interpretation of the films selected. Admittedly he is fulsome in his praise of the technical innovations achieved by Weimar's directors and he has done much to establish the canonical films of the era, but increasingly this work must be viewed with a certain care.

Lotte Eisner's *The Haunted Screen* approaches the era from an art-history perspective. It locates the films within a continuity of artistic and literary predecessors, where the work of the expressionist theatre is a powerful influence upon the films of the early Weimar years.

> The leaning towards violent contrast – which in Expressionist literature can be seen in the use of staccato sentences – and the inborn German liking for chiaroscuro and shadow, obviously found an ideal artistic outlet in the cinema. Visions nourished by moods of vague and troubled yearning could have found no more apt mode of expression, at once concrete and unreal. (1969: 17)

Eisner does not regard this fact in entirely positive terms, but she successfully illustrates the debt owed by German film to its theatrical and literary predecessors, drawing upon Romanticism and the German fascination with the *unheimlich* in particular. She also attributes much of expressionist cinema's unique *mise-en-scène* to the work of the theatre director Max Reinhardt who, as director of the influential *Deutsches Theater* in Berlin, provided the young film industry with a great many of its key personnel in the postwar era. Of Weimar's brief flowering and rapid decline she comments laconically (but significantly) 'It is not easy to find a dream again once the spell is broken' (1969: 311).

Decades after these two texts had served to establish German Expressionism as one of the most dynamic cinematic movements in the early history of film, Elsaesser has proposed a revised view of these two works, which certainly does not seek to remove either from their respective pedestals as seminal texts of German film studies but equally suggests that they have lost some validity in the intervening years:

> Their works, more than any other, have encouraged a potent analogy between film culture and political history, where experience (of key films) so uncannily matches expectation (of what German cinema should 'reflect') that the convergence of image with its object has for nearly fifty years seemed all but self-evident. (2000a: 3)

Elsaesser acknowledges the 'appropriately lurid and brilliantly suggestive titles' (2000a: 20) of Kracauer's and Eisner's books, before going on to suggest that both authors reflect aspects of what he now describes as the 'historical imaginary' of film in the Weimar Republic; or, rather, of the 'two imaginaries' (2000a: 34) which highlight the inherent contradictions and tensions in these films, at once making a study of Weimar cinema so challenging and so frustrating:

> If their [Kracauer and Eisner] underlying assumptions have become questionable to film historians, they did grasp what for several generations of viewers has rendered this cinema distinctive: its Janus-faced ambivalences, its journeys into the interior of cultural Modernism, some of whose intellectual *tours de force* the films enthusiastically perform at the same time as they eclectically transform them. The blend of sophistication and sensationalism, of art and kitsch, the exploration of pathological perception and psychic borderline states make many of the films produced between 1919 and 1929 into historical documents precisely where they appear most fictional, fantastic and ahistorical. (2000a: 34–5)

Indicative perhaps of the enduring appeal of Weimar cinema is the fact that these three authors are by no means the only authorities in the field, even if they must be regarded as major figures. There are studies by pioneers of film criticism and film history such as Paul Rotha's *The Film 'Til Now* (1930), through to the detailed examinations of specific genres and films by the likes of Paul Coates (*The Gorgon's Gaze: German Cinema, Expressionism, and the Legacy of Horror*, 1991) or the exhaustive account of the history of

Ufa by Klaus Kreimeier, *The Ufa-Story: A History of Germany's Greatest Film Company 1918–1945* (1999), all of which demonstrate the range of critical work addressing this subject.[7]

The perennial appeal of Expressionism

After initial resistance to German films in the first postwar years, particularly in Britain, France and the USA,[8] they quickly gained in popularity at home and abroad. Whilst part of that success may be explained purely in economic terms (high inflation in Germany meant that the films were relatively cheap to make and export and the currency they earned abroad was of particular value for the same reason), it is quite clear that the German film industry quickly hit upon a radical, anti-realist approach to filmmaking which transcended any lingering national antipathies. Quite simply, the best films of the era are breathtaking in their conception, innovative in their execution and utterly compelling in their narratives. Kreimeier refers to the 'magic kitchen' of Ufa, where 'writers, directors, actors, cameramen, and set designers conjured up magical worlds ... producing film fantasies throughout the 1920s, symphonies of weightless matter, of light, shadow, and iridescent movement' (1999: 4). Erich Pommer, the producer who possibly deserves most credit for Germany's success abroad, at times underplays the collaborative effort of the filmmakers, recalling that much which made the Weimar film unique was as a result of exigencies of the time; perhaps a shortage of electricity, the natural tendency of the Reinhardt-trained actors to exaggerate their gestures, or simply the opportunity to make a film quickly and economically (see Robinson 1997: 11). Elsewhere, though, it is clear that the Weimar system was essentially a creative powerhouse, typically based around the 'director-unit'. This close-knit, collaborative approach led rivals at times to marvel at Germany's mastery of the medium. After the premiere of Murnau's *The Last Laugh* in the United States, Karl Freund recalls the reaction of one US studio:

> There was a telegram from Hollywood addressed to Ufa, asking what camera we had used to shoot the film. It added that in the USA there was no such camera, and no town to compare with the one in our film. The Americans, used to a precise technique, didn't dream that we had discovered new methods with only the most primitive means at our disposal. (quoted in Eisner 1973: 65–7)

Although not all films were instant hits, at home or abroad, the benefit of some eighty years of hindsight confirms that at their best, the films selected here – as well as many others from the period – have a visual daring and a dazzling luminosity which shines through even today.

Thus this dedicated and talented group of filmmakers devised a fundamentally new mode of presentation, creating dream worlds where light and darkness were carefully controlled, which established the reputation of the Weimar film industry for perpetuity. They drew on an art form with which they would have been well-familiar to deliver a dazzling display for this still-young medium. As historian Rainer Metzger commented:

> [Expressionism] always set its sights on tumultuousness and fragmentation, on separation and collision, and right to the last moment it poured out its heart and soul in the search for a language to convey violent and nervous exertion. (2007: 78)

In the expressionist cinema of the Weimar Republic the chosen language was visual: ironically, even as Expressionism in its various other guises expired, its brief cinematic revival provided the world with some of the movement's most abiding images, which themselves are now considered synonymous with the chaotic period of the Weimar Republic.

2 AUTHORITY OVERTHROWN, *OR* LUNATICS IN THE ASYLUM: ROBERT WIENE'S *DAS CABINET DES DR CALIGARI*

Given the impact of Expressionism on the cultural scene in Germany before World War One, it seems strange that the cinema only really fixed on the movement in the years immediately after Germany's defeat. Still more surprising is that the move appears, on one level at least, to have been almost an accidental decision to shoot a film containing elements of the visually striking art. In this chapter we will examine some of the factors which influenced the style of the film credited with launching the era of expressionist cinema, Robert Wiene's *The Cabinet of Dr Caligari*. When *Dr Caligari* was released in February 1920 its astonishing set design immediately caught the attention of the critic and the filmgoer alike. Although it should be reiterated that such designs were not uncommon in pre-war expressionist art and on the expressionist stage, the startling zigzags, the swirling arabesques and the outrageously exaggerated furniture which created the world within which the actors moved were a novelty in film at the time, and must have gone a long way to establishing the film's fame upon its release. Many other films then copied this design element, albeit in a less frantic manner, in an attempt to recreate the sense of disjuncture which was so admirably evoked by the jagged rooftops of Holstenwall. To contemporary reviewers it was quite apparent that this film heralded a new era in filmmaking.

What is not clear, however, is exactly how the filmmakers came to make this film (which might otherwise have been fairly unremarkable) in such an iconographic style – not least because, as has already been pointed out, Expressionism in other areas of cultural production was all but dead in

1920. There can be no doubt that for narratives of authority abused (not to mention the portrayal of murder, twilight dreams and the descent into madness), the expressionist tradition would provide a rich vein of imagery. But what remains unclear is how Expressionism found its way into German films at this time. Whereas expressionist painting, for example, made great use of strong colours and ambitious palettes, the filmmakers who took up the standard of Expressionism in the 1920s faced a huge and obvious restriction: they could only shoot in black and white.[1] Undaunted by this apparent problem, the early films relied upon many of the practices and conventions of the earlier expressionist theatre to stimulate and to provoke. Thus the *mise-en-scène* of the expressionist films sought to add colour through the broader imagery portrayed onscreen. Lotte Eisner traces the artistic and theatrical influences which had the greatest impact on the major films of the Weimar era, although she is candid in admitting that an exact definition of Expressionism in film is likely to be impossible. Instead she points out that *Der Student von Prag* (*The Student of Prague*, Paul Wegener, 1913) already displays most of the elements to be observed in German expressionist films from *Dr Caligari* onwards, namely 'that preoccupation with setting and atmosphere which was to be characteristic of the entire German cinema' (1969: 43).

But this principle at least partly explains why German expressionist films often seem so slow, even compared to other silent movies of the 1920s, since the compositional element required more time on screen than was perhaps the case in other 'national' cinemas. Likewise, this explains why the camera was (at least initially) reluctant to move in expressionist films since, again, it is considerably more difficult to maintain the composition of a shot if the camera is tracking across a set. Finally, the compositional element outlined here explains why the behaviour of the actors in many expressionist films comes across as stilted. Notwithstanding the legacy of the expressionist movement on stage – advocating exaggerated gestures as a complement to the nature of the narrative – actors in expressionist films found themselves subordinated to the films' visuals, their characters literally part of the decoration. In this sense they were required to do little more than glide across the set in a manner which would harmonise with the set design.

And then there is the lighting. One feature particularly characteristic of many expressionist sets in the early phase of Weimar cinema is the use of painted effects to create the impression of light and shadow, and, indeed, the use of artificial lighting in preference to natural light sources. In *Dr Caligari* in particular, shadows are painted onto the flats which form the walls of the town or the various interior locations, and even across floors and up and down staircases. Even where a real (nevertheless artificial!) form of lighting was utilised, this effect was often enhanced by painted shadows: a form of 'hyper-expressionism' which came close to achieving the pre-war expressionists' goal of heightened reality. Light and darkness in *Dr Caligari* and other films of the era operated simultaneously as a signifier as well as the signified, playing the role of a delineating function in liminal spaces which mapped the boundaries between dream and the waking state, the conscious and the subconscious.

Thus a film such as *Dr Caligari* which sought to portray the descent into madness of an individual fighting an authoritarian, Machiavellian figure, required a set which would enhance that sense of a mind unbalanced. Contemporary German audiences would have been entirely comfortable with the use of such stylised sets in plays of the day. Not only Max Reinhardt's troupe but virtually every theatre of note would have included some expressionist plays in its repertoire, and some theatres specialised in the anti-authoritarian plays of Ernst Toller, Carl Sternheim and others. Indeed, the likes of Werner Krauss and Conrad Veidt had appeared in many of the most celebrated expressionist productions in the preceding years. Just before filming began on *Dr Caligari* they had appeared in Reinhold Goering's *Seeschlacht*, which ran during the winter of 1918/19 at the *Deutsches Theater* in Berlin (see Robinson 1997: 40). All that was required was a decision to employ the style of one of these plays in a film.

Robert Wiene – the father of German expressionist film?

Perhaps owing to Kracauer's seminal *From Caligari to Hitler*, the very title of which posits a causal link between Wiene's infamous character and the horrors of the Nazis, *Dr Caligari* is possibly the most widely known film of the Weimar period. Yet compared to his contemporaries, until recently relatively little had been known about this director's life. This has been rectified by the archival research of Uli Jung and Walter Schatzberg (1999), and the restoration efforts of several prominent film archives around the world.

Robert Wiene was born on 27 April 1873 in Breslau (then part of Prussia), the oldest of two boys (his brother Conrad was born in 1878, and became a film director in his own right). His father Carl pursued a successful theatrical career as an actor culminating at the Royal Court Theatre in Dresden. Initially Wiene chose to study law in Berlin and Vienna between 1894–96, but this period also saw a growing interest in art. He began practising law in Vienna, yet by 1908 Wiene was the business director of the *Kleines Schauspielhaus* theatre in the city, possibly thanks to his father's contacts. He must have started to write film scripts around this time, though, because by 1912 his first screenplay – entitled *Die Waffe der Jugend* (*The Weapons of Youth*) – was filmed. (It may also have been directed by Wiene, but it has not survived.) He then accepted a contract with the Messter Film Company[2] and was involved as writer and/or director in over thirty films in the period 1914–19. It seems that Wiene had established himself as an eminently respected member of the industry by the end of World War One. Such was his reputation that the release of *Satanas* in 1919, which had in actual fact been directed by the still relatively unknown F. W. Murnau, was instead associated with Wiene, who had merely acted in the capacity of artistic supervisor. Immediately after working on *Satanas*, Wiene began shooting the film which was to establish his reputation as the father of German expressionist film.

Years later Fritz Lang claimed that he had turned down the opportunity to direct *Dr Caligari*, and indeed that he was responsible for proposing the use of the framing story in the film, which we shall discuss shortly (see also McGilligan 1997); but for whatever reason it was Wiene who was given the project and what seems quite apparent now is that the film in its final, unique form was in no small measure due to the influence of Robert Wiene in collaboration with the team he assembled to make it.

Dr Caligari premièred at the Berlin Marmorhaus on 27 February 1920 to almost universal acclaim, at home and abroad (see Robinson 1997: 46–7). Looking back on the period, the influential critic Paul Rotha pronounced the film 'a drop of wine in an ocean of salt water', dismissing such celebrated classics as D. W. Griffith's *The Birth of a Nation* (1915), as 'negligible when compared with the possibilities laid bare by *Das Cabinet des Dr Caligari*' (1967: 93–4). Rotha's opinion seems to have shaped the film's reception ever since: 'It is destined to go down to posterity as one of the two most momentous advances achieved by any one film in the history of the development of the cinema till now' (1967: 94).[3]

Following its enormous success, Wiene's career went from strength to strength, and he produced a further dozen or so films up to the beginning of the 1930s. Both *Genuine* (1920), and *Raskolnikow* (1923) were filmed in a similar expressionist style to the first hit, albeit with less success. The formula was repeated one last time when Conrad Veidt played a concert pianist who is tormented when, after an accident, he receives the transplanted hands of a murderer in *Orlacs Hände* (*The Hands of Orlac*, 1924).

Returning to Vienna, Wiene then directed a film version of Richard Strauss's *Der Rosenkavalier* (1925) to great acclaim: by this time his reputation proved a guarantee of both critical and commercial success and he even took the advent of the talkies in his stride. Films such as *Der Andere* (*The Other*, 1930),[4] a Jekyll and Hyde story starring Fritz Kortner (the banker besotted with Louise Brooks in Pabst's *Pandora's Box*; see chapter 5), and the gangster adventure *Panik in Chicago* (1931) were particularly praised. One critic opined: 'Robert Wiene, the master director of silent film, has also conquered the word' (cited in Jung & Schatzberg 1999: 155).

The rise of Hitler curtailed this success. Wiene's last film to be made in Germany, *Taifun* (*Typhoon*, 1933), was banned by the authorities, and he chose to move abroad to continue his career. By 1934 he was working on a long-planned project to shoot a talking version of *Dr Caligari* in Britain, but never realised this dream. Instead he shot a film entitled *Ultimatum* in France in 1938, which starred Erich von Stroheim (an established actor and director in his own right, following films such as *Greed* – which he had directed in 1924 – and *La Grande illusion* (Jean Renoir, 1937). Like Renoir's classic, with which it was compared, *Ultimatum* depicted the events leading up to the outbreak of World War One in humanistic terms, depicting a Serbian army officer and an Austrian woman, whose love is torn apart by nationalism and the lust for war.

Wiene did not complete the shoot of *Ultimatum*. A rare photo from the set shows the normally rotund director looking gaunt and tired (Jung & Schatzberg 1999: 186). He had accepted the project against medical advice, and this, coupled perhaps with the stress of exile, had taken its toll. In the final days of filming he collapsed, and died in hospital on 15 July 1938. In the introduction to their comprehensive account of his life, Jung and Schatzberg sum up his talent:

Wiene comes across as a competent, versatile and sought-after director, who again and again had to balance the commercial and artistic
aspects of his work. As far as we can gather ... Wiene's commercial
films from the 1920s are tasteful mass products. (1999: xiii)

Although F. W. Murnau died earlier (see chapter 3), Wiene was the oldest
of those who form what might be regarded as the central group of major
Weimar directors.[5] It is fitting that his reputation, for so long based solely
upon the phenomenon of *Dr Caligari*, is now being examined in the light of
his prodigious output, literally to the moment he died.

The Cabinet of Dr Caligari: putting it all together[6]

Few films which aspire to a place in the pantheon of innovative movie-
making can have been as dogged by controversy as *The Cabinet of Dr
Caligari*. In the years following its success everyone involved with the
project wanted to take the credit for its groundbreaking visual style. Thus
it is illuminating to examine the claims that various individuals have made
that they provided the creative impetus behind *Dr Caligari*'s unique *mise-
en-scène*; a stylistic approach which has become the trademark of Weimar
film. Only Wiene himself seems to have remained silent over this issue of
who was responsible for the advent of Expressionism in film.

The film's producer at Decla Bioscop, Erich Pommer (who became head
of production at Ufa when it bought out Decla in 1923), was less interested
in *Dr Caligari*'s expressionist credentials, except inasmuch as it was a
crucial factor in the film's positive critical reception. He claimed to have
recognised its box office appeal, and the relative cost-effectiveness of its
mise-en-scène, from the moment the scriptwriters Hans Janowitz and Carl
Mayer walked into his office: 'They saw in their script an "Experiment" – I
saw a comparatively inexpensive production' (quoted in Robinson 1997:
11). Although various accounts contradict themselves, crucially casting
doubt that any one testimony is wholly reliable, the set designers, led by
Hermann Warm, subsequently recalled conversations amongst the creative team in the pre-production phase before shooting commenced, during
which time they overcame Wiene's initial objections to the appropriation
of expressionist urban designs. Furthermore, the film's scriptwriters, both
of whom had suffered in their own way through the horrors of the war,

Caligari's cabinet:
a world of sleep-
walkers and insanity

went on to claim that they had set out to make a film which would be a perfect call to anti-authoritarianism. Their message, so they claimed, was emasculated by Robert Wiene's unnecessary application of the framing story. Whereas they had proposed a revolutionary story of authority over-thrown, Wiene's realisation of *Dr Caligari* was rather a reactionary tale of authority reasserting itself, and thereby re-establishing order out of chaos – the threat of anarchy being a particularly resonant theme in Germany and German films at this time.[7] In the twelve months leading up to the film's première, much had happened to convince ordinary Germans that a monumental struggle between bitter political rivals was taking place, with economic chaos and armed uprisings being very much the order of the day. This served to ensure that the audiences which went to see the film were thoroughly sensitised to its depiction of authority, revolution and counter-revolution.[8]

The plot of *Dr Caligari* is, on the surface at least, deceptively simple: a professor (Werner Krauss), the director of a mental institute close to the fictitious town of Holstenwall, has learned of a particular form of ancient hypnotism through the writings of a sixteenth-century Italian doctor called Caligari. He thus masters the technique in order to control the somnam-bulist Cesare (Conrad Veidt), whom he displays to a fee-paying public at a fair in the town. But the power this mountebank wields over Cesare allows him to manipulate the somnambulist into committing a series of murders. Franzis (Friedrich Feher) is the friend of one of Cesare's victims, and fiancé of Jane (Lil Dagover), who is subsequently abducted by the somnambulist. He unmasks the director (whose character seems to be merged with, or possessed by, the ancient Caligari) and confines him within his own institute. But then, in an unexpected twist it transpires that it is Franzis, not Caligari, who is deranged, that the events of the film are consequently the product of Franzis's weakened mind, and that Caligari is a benign director after all. The film ends with the Doctor's authority restored and with his pledge to rehabilitate Franzis the madman. Thus, the reliability of virtually everything the audience has previously witnessed is called into question by the closing minutes of the action. How much of the story actually happened? How much is intended to be read as no more than a figment of the madman's imagination? What is the name of the asylum director, if not Caligari? Is he even the same character as the fairground showman? And will Franzis replace Cesare as Caligari's puppet? This confusion has enhanced the film's reputation, but has simultaneously been responsible for the disagreements ever since over the film's real meaning.

From the earliest days of the film's success, Hans Janowitz and Carl Mayer maintained that their script was a perfect account of authority overthrown. They accused Wiene of exercising a cowardly form of self-censorship, by adding the framing story which sees Caligari's power restored, thereby attenuating the apparently anti-authoritarian message of the original script in order to placate Pommer and the studio. Their case was taken up enthusiastically by Siegfried Kracauer, the better to support the central thesis of his study of Weimar films:

> Janowitz and Mayer … raged against the framing story [because] it perverted, if not reversed, their intrinsic intentions. While the original story exposed the madness inherent in authority, Wiene's Caligari glorified authority and convicted its antagonist of madness. A revolutionary film was thus turned into a conformist one … This change undoubtedly resulted not so much from Wiene's personal predilections as from his instinctive submission to the necessities of the screen; films, at least commercial ones, are forced to answer to mass desires. (1947: 67)

Kracauer's accusation may seem, at one level, justified: it is surely not at all unreasonable for Wiene to have paid close attention to the wishes of the audience, since these, after all, were the constraints imposed upon a commercial venture such as a film, not least in the economic climate prevailing in the early years of Weimar's fledgling democracy. Furthermore, the film's box office success would seem to vindicate his decision. In fact, Wiene not only knew exactly what he was doing when he chose to excise elements of the script but also produced a better film for it. Moreover, his directorial input, ensuring that the revised story-frame should be echoed in repeated circular imagery (in a film better known for its harsh angles and jagged lighting effects), points towards a very deliberate attempt to reflect the pattern of events unfolding on Germany's streets. If the motifs of cycle and revolution which feature throughout the film are taken into account, the narrative frame offers a far more sinister interpretation.[9] These motifs serve as indicators that Wiene clearly had it in mind to offer a representation of the reactionary events of recent German history, a history which saw authority overthrown in 1918 – in the form of the abdication of the *Kaiser*, and the attempted regulation of the generals – but reinstated in the chaotic early days of the Weimar Republic. The spirits in the opening framing story can be read as the anti-democratic, reactionary forces which were all too real in the lives of *Dr Caligari*'s audience in Weimar.

Caligari: madman or guarantor of stability?

Elements of the cycle are thus artfully accentuated at regular intervals throughout the film but nowhere more so, perhaps, than at the Holstenwall fairground which occupies a key position in the film. In every scene portraying the fair there are images of revolution and cycle in abundance. The fairground carousels (themselves patently artificial constructions), which are erected against the two-dimensional backdrop of the sets, spin crazily and ceaselessly. At the same time, a real merry-go-round turns in the middle distance, while an organ-grinder is observed labouring at his machine in order to elicit a few coins from the passers-by.[10] As the citizens of an unsuspecting Holstenwall wander around the fair, the image is one of vitality and life but one which also prefigures chaos and, as in the medieval *Totentanz*, one which ultimately leads to death.[11] Thus it is highly appropriate that Caligari unleashes his instrument of murder from a fair, since it is here that the elemental cycle of life is completed. Kracauer identified the fair as 'an enclave of anarchy in the sphere of entertainment' and the imagery of the carousels as the epitome of this: 'The circle here becomes a symbol of chaos' (1947: 73–4).[12] Thus the fair acts as the chaotic counterpoint to order and freedom, offering a barely-coded reference to events on the streets of Berlin and elsewhere. But whilst the script envisaged early scenes of labourers erecting stalls and booths at the fair before inviting the audience to observe Dr Caligari's awe-inspiring (and fear-inducing) act, Wiene opts instead to focus solely on the scenes of chaos and revolution, before ushering the audience into the tent which contains the mysterious cabinet.

Taken in this light the imagery of the town of Holstenwall can be seen to reinforce the cyclical element of the film. Although the painted backdrop of the town can be regarded as a conglomeration of Expressionism and Brueghel-like constriction, and although the individual scenes display the painted shadows and jagged rooftops for which the film would become famous, the repetition of the loci, with characters constantly returning to the same spot, serves to reinforce the notion of cycle and revolution. Like Franz Kafka's celebrated protagonist Josef K., a literary contemporary of the hapless Franzis,[13] Wiene's characters are condemned to scuttle around the labyrinthine streets of Holstenwall, facing imperious petty bureaucrats and seemingly incapable of escape. Here, too, Wiene's decision to open the tale with a conversation on a bench, which is only later revealed to be within the walls of the lunatic asylum, can now be understood as a significant underscoring of the central message: resistance is doomed to failure, escape apparently impossible. Thereafter, when the *mise-en-scène* of the mental institute is examined, the interpretation of *Dr Caligari* as a film focused on revolution is complete. It may be observed that Franzis stands at the centre of a spiral pattern painted on the floor of the institute, at the point in the film where Caligari is overthrown. Possibly this denotes the focus of Franzis's life, with opportunities and possibilities radiating away from him. Or perhaps the spiral pattern may be viewed as symbolic of his mental degradation, swirling in confusion, and leading him to the sorry state seen at the end of the film. But a further examination of cycle and revolution in the film demands an alternative reading. It is at this location, after all, that the wheel turns full circle, for this is the place where the attempt to unmask and overthrow the Doctor is defeated, the point at which Caligari regains his position of ascendancy. Instead of an expressionistic device standing as a cipher for instability and madness, the mental institute becomes instead the focal point for a different kind of instability, namely that of political revolution, and the scene of the triumph of reactionary forces – something which comes extraordinarily close to true events in Weimar Germany at the time.

The success of *The Cabinet of Dr Caligari* established a reputation for German film throughout Europe and the USA which became both a blessing and a curse.[14] Thanks to the general appreciation of the film's radical *mise-en-scène*, German filmmakers henceforth enjoyed greater access to foreign markets which were warmly appreciative of the prestige and cachet of exclusivity or otherness brought by German films. It also helped to establish film as a medium in Germany which could increasingly be considered on a par with the more established arts of German cultural life. But it also acted as something of a straitjacket (rather appropriate given the nature of the film's conclusion), condemning German film to generic and stylistic expectations which it embraced enthusiastically. At the very least, *Dr Caligari* paved the way for a whole legion of German film émigrés – directors, cameramen, set designers and scriptwriters – who would subsequently make the journey across the Atlantic into economic, and later political, exile. What started perhaps as little more than an exercise in financial exigency, or an attempt to give postwar film some legitimacy, coupled with innovative *mise-en-scène*, resulted in a uniquely stylised set design, the employment of painted *chiaroscuro* effects and the adoption of an exaggerated acting method, which in turn established the reputation of Weimar film and thereby represented and perpetuated German Expressionism for at least a decade.

The knock-on effect of filmic Expressionism, triggered by *Dr Caligari*'s international success, cannot be underestimated: for almost a decade the majority of German films were shot entirely on set. Even films which featured scenes supposedly played out in the open air eschewed external locations in favour of huge sets constructed in Ufa's Neubabelsberg studio, and elsewhere. Robert Wiene's later film *INRI* (1923), for instance, which features Christ's Sermon on the Mount, was shot on a hill made entirely of timber, beneath banks of arc lighting on gantries high in the roof of the huge Staaken sheds in Berlin, which had formerly housed zeppelins. Likewise, the primeval forest scenes in Fritz Lang's *Die Nibelungen* (to be examined in chapter 5) were filmed on studio lots with trees constructed from cement pasted onto wire armatures. Even in the later years of the Weimar period, when location shooting began to gain favour, directors such as Lang would think of nothing of rearranging nature to make it more natural in their eyes (see Kreimeier 1999: 106).

Where these later expressionist films differ in their lighting is that the early, bold experiment of painted lighting effects quickly gave way to greater experimentation with artificial light sources. Was production kept indoors to allow greater control over lighting or did the lighting techniques develop because location shooting was not favoured by the Weimar directors? Either way, it is perhaps for their lighting that German expressionist films became best known, although the whole package of *mise-en-scène* elements combined to stun observers of Weimar film and to establish the reputation of German film worldwide as a cinema fundamentally devoted to artistic goals. Whoever was responsible for the decision to shoot *The Cabinet of Dr Caligari* in an expressionist style, and whether that decision was taken by accident or design, Wiene and his team established a template for filming the themes and motifs which preoccupied Weimar cinema for the best part of a decade. As filmmakers portrayed ghouls and monsters, explored liminal states and oneric visions and proferred depictions of Germany's past and future, the ability to depict the inner machinations of the individual's mind by means of filmic Expressionism was both timely and hugely successful, at home and abroad.

3   DEMONS WITHOUT AND WITHIN: F. W. MURNAU'S
NOSFERATU

Its unusual *mise-en-scène* notwithstanding, the success of *The Cabinet of Dr Caligari* can be attributed in great measure to the air of abnormality which permeated its imagery. The sense of unease, of a creepy, uncanny atmosphere intruding into quotidian life is summed up by the German term *unheimlich*, a concept which has a long literary and artistic tradition in German culture. The well-known Grimm brothers' *Kinder- und Hausmärchen (Children's and Household Tales)* of 1812, for instance, seem to confirm that the stories most beloved of the Germans are those which are filled with ghouls and witches, threatening to abduct, boil, eat or otherwise do harm to the human characters. Such well-known tales as Little Red Riding Hood or Hansel and Gretel (just two of those recorded by the brothers), amply demonstrate how the nation's dark forests go hand-in-hand with tales of horror and the paranormal.

Following on from the military defeat of Germany in 1918, the young Weimar Republic suffered an inauspicious start. Not only had millions died as a result of the conflict, but thousands more were killed in three outbreaks of Spanish influenza which swept across Europe between 1917 and 1919.[1] Furthermore, the reparations forced upon Germany by the victorious Allies at Versailles in June 1919 extended the misery: short-lived revolutions, the French occupation of the Ruhr and street fighting between rival factions became part of the daily struggle to survive. Hyper-inflation and mass-unemployment followed, resulting in individuals wheeling around barrow-loads of cash in the search for a loaf of bread, and unemployed former soldiers standing in line for a bowl of soup. Little wonder, then,

The epitome of
horror: F. W. Murnau's
'nosferatu' monster

that narratives of foreboding, images of ghouls and other horrors, and
psychological studies of the beast within struck a nerve with a population
which was, metaphorically at least, still glancing over its shoulder in fear,
uncertain of its future in a period of chaos.

As Lotte Eisner illustrated admirably in her work *The Haunted Screen*
German art and literature offered ample images of horror for the citizens
of the Republic, images which filmmakers were quick to appropriate.
The Romantics' celebration of the *unheimlich* and the supernatural lent
German film what Siegfried Prawer calls the 'rich heritage of demonic folklore, Gothic fiction, and black Romanticism' (1980: 32) which seemingly
lies at the heart of German culture.

In Expressionism there was a mixed reaction to the supernatural, since
many in the movement were more concerned with invisible terrors than the
inner conflicts and emotions of the individual. Edvard Munch's *The Scream*
(1893) perfectly encapsulates the expressionist belief that horror is not
solely the result of external terrors. Even so, the expressionist filmmakers
quickly discovered that there was a lucrative market for fear in postwar
Germany.

Even though it would be entirely misleading to claim that the paranormal and the supernatural were the only themes in early German film, the number of surviving films and titles do suggest that this was a popular genre in the years before and after World War One.[2] Thus *Das Todestelephon* (*The Telephone of Death*, Oskar Messter, 1912), *Die Insel der Seligen* (*The Island of the Dead*, Max Reinhardt, 1913) or *Der Andere* (*The Other*, Max Mack, 1913), to mention just three, all dealt with themes of terror and the paranormal to a certain extent: *The Other*, for instance, was a Jekyll and Hyde tale of one man's struggle to contain his alter ego and the ensuing fight between good and evil. It became apparent that horror was able to pay its way, establishing a generic expectation which, when coupled with a renowned director and/or a star lead, could reasonably expect to make a profit both in Berlin and elsewhere.

Paul Wegener: 'the father of Caligari'

An early success in this genre came with *Der Student von Prag* (*The Student of Prague*, 1913), a script written and directed by the young Reinhardt actor Paul Wegener, co-directed with Stellan Rye. Produced by Deutsche Bioscop (which was later responsible for *The Cabinet of Dr Caligari*), it was based on Goethe's archetypally Germanic version of the *Faust* legend, as well as material by E. T. A. Hoffmann. The film was a chilling tale of one man's descent into madness. More importantly, it paved the way for a series of horror movies in Germany and laid down the marker for a visual style which we would now consider typical of expressionist film. As Paul Cooke claims: 'If *Caligari* is the father of [cinematic] Expressionism, *Der Student von Prag* can be seen as the father of *Caligari*' (2002: 20).

In the film, Balduin, the eponymous student of Prague (played by Wegener), has crippling debts, and develops an infatuation with the noblewoman Countess Margit (Grete Berger). In desperation he turns to the satanic wizard Scapinelli (John Gottowt) who agrees to solve all the young man's woes, in return for anything in Balduin's possession. Balduin accepts and Scapinelli claims the young student's reflection as payment. Although the young man's fortunes in life and love do indeed improve, he is tormented by his *Doppelgänger* (who, in the classic psychoanalytical sense, can be viewed as Balduin's repressed desires made incarnate), until his alter ego eventually implicates him in murder. The desperate student attempts to shoot his evil double, but instead succeeds only in shooting himself. As he dies, Scapinelli mocks him, scattering the torn pieces of their contract over his body. In the final scene Balduin's tormenting alter ego stands over the unfortunate's grave. A lacklustre remake of *The Student of Prague* in 1926[3] shows just how quickly the genre developed in the first decades of the industry's history, quickly becoming a staple part of a moviegoer's diet.[4]

Buoyed by the success of *The Student of Prague*, Wegener returned to the world of horror and the supernatural to produce and star in *Der Golem* (*The Golem*, Henrik Galeen, 1915). Again based on a mixture of sources and drawing heavily on Jewish mythology, the story of the Golem was one of man's desire to exert control over others, on the one hand, and of a mistrust of artificial lifeforms, on the other. These are of course themes which recur regularly throughout the Weimar period (see the section on *Metropolis* in the next chapter, for instance), and indeed continue to be popular to this day. This film, too, was remade just a few years later as *Der Golem, wie er in die Welt kam* (*The Golem, How He Came Into the World*, Paul Wegener and Carl Boese, 1920). The earlier version is now lost, but the remake, which is still available, reveals just how neatly this story fits into the overall pattern of supernatural films.

The Golem is a clay automaton, created to meet a specific need at a time of testing. The Lord of a medieval German city intends to banish the Jewish population, so old Rabbi Löw (Albert Steinrück) turns to cabbalistic texts in his search for a solution. From these texts he learns how to create a magical homunculus, a clay statue which will carry out the rabbi's wishes without hesitation. Initially all goes well and the Golem is instrumental in restoring the fortunes of the Jews. Later, however, the Golem abducts the rabbi's daughter Miriam (Lyda Salmanova), and then rampages through the city streets. Only an encounter with a little girl eventually stays his hand. Thus beguiled, the Golem cannot prevent the girl from removing the life-giving key from his chest, whereupon he reverts to clay and the terror is ended.[5] A series of six films in Germany, the first part entitled *Homunculus* (Otto Rippert, 1916) likewise took up the theme of the clay monster with great success.

But not only does the success of such films suggest, that the topic was one dear to the hearts of the German audience, it is also clear that the *unheimliche Stimmung*, or unsettling atmosphere of these tales provided creative impetus to filmmakers still seeking to establish the cinema as a legitimate art form. Furthermore, such films were equally successful from a commercial point of view. Wegener himself later explained how the genre established itself for both commercial and technical reasons:

> After a few failed films, about which I would rather remain silent, I had the idea of the Golem, this strange, mythical clay figure of the Rabbi Löw from the legends of the Prague ghetto, and with this I moved still further into the territory of the purely filmic – here everything is presented on the screen, in a flowing together of a fantasy world of previous centuries with present-day life. (Quoted in Scherber 1990: 27)

Thus the screen became the perfect medium to combine elements of Romanticism, the Gothic novel and other artistic influences with the population's day to day fears over the volatile political situation in Weimar Germany. Utilising expressionist effects to the full, filmmakers succeeded in articulating a sense of existential angst before psychoanalysis had reached the popular consciousness. Artistic integrity and box-office success seemed to go hand-in-hand and the genre flourished. Still more significant from the point of view of this study was Wegener's realisation that the medium allowed for new narrative possibilities, particularly in the area of lighting, which could be utilised to enhance the sense of foreboding in the audience, sitting as it was in a darkened room: 'Rhythm and tempo, light and dark all play a role in film just like in music' (ibid.). The fantastic, the subconscious, the dream world and the horrific – all summed up in one way or another by the term *unheimlich* – discovered a natural home in early cinema. Siegfried Kracauer goes so far as to suggest that this theme was particularly apt for the early filmmakers since it presented them with technological challenges which would serve to set the cinema apart from other artistic media (1947: 28f).

F. W. Murnau and Nosferatu

Of all the films which sought to depict the pervasive fear of the German people as the Republic lurched from one crisis to the next, the 'symphony of horror' called *Nosferatu* is surely the best known. Its director, F. W.

Murnau was described by Lotte Eisner as 'the greatest film-director the Germans have ever known', claiming that in his films 'cinematic composition was never a mere attempt at decorative stylization. He created the most overwhelming and poignant images in the whole German cinema' (1969: 97).

Murnau was born Friedrich Wilhelm Plumpe on 28 December 1888, into a respectable middle-class family in Kassel. Whilst at university in Berlin and Heidelberg, and in defiance of his father's plans for him, he fell in with a group of young, avant-garde artists, including the poet Else Lasker-Schüler, who had contributed greatly to the expressionist scene in Berlin, and Franz Marc, the founder of the 'Blue Rider' group in Munich (see chapter 1). Inspired by these vivacious young people he changed his name to Murnau, after the Bavarian spa village where they vacationed together, and pursued his real love of acting. He was discovered by Max Reinhardt and began his theatrical training at the *Deutsches Theater* in Berlin, where he became acquainted with the likes of Emil Jannings, Werner Krauss and, a particular friend, Conrad Veidt.

Murnau volunteered for military service in 1914 and served, first as an infantry officer on the Eastern Front, then as an observer in a *Luftwaffe* squadron in France, where he reputedly survived a number of crashes. In 1917 he and his pilot are supposed to have inadvertently flown across the Swiss border, where they landed and were interned by the neutral authorities there. Murnau saw out the rest of the war in relative comfort, even directing some stage plays to general acclaim from local critics. Murnau later recalled that he was also approached by the German Embassy in Switzerland to produce propaganda films for the German war effort. Nothing remains of them today to confirm Murnau's anecdote.

After repatriation Murnau renewed his association with the Reinhardt actors. Instead of returning to the stage, however, he founded a film production company with Conrad Veidt called the *Murnau Veidt Filmgesellschaft* and began making films. Significantly, the supernatural and the uncanny seem to have been staple motifs of much of Murnau's early film production. His first film *Der blaue Junge* (*The Blue Boy*, 1919) depicts a nobleman's struggle to rid himself of a curse, which centres on a portrait of the eponymous blue boy hanging in the familial home. Later films continue the theme: *Der Januskopf* (*The Head of Janus*, 1920) is a variation on the Jekyll and Hyde story, and supernatural elements can be observed too in *Schloss*

Vogelöd (*The Haunted Castle*, 1921) and *Phantom* (1922). Murnau's international breakthrough came in 1925 with the release of *The Last Laugh*. In this film of social status and degradation, the senior porter of a metropolitan hotel (played by Emil Jannings) is demoted and loses his standing and self-respect as a result. The film charts his steady decline until, in a curious – and barely credible – reversal of fortune, a millionaire bequeaths him a fortune and he returns to the hotel, this time as a guest where he can exact revenge of a sort by treating his best friend to a marvellous meal whilst his former manager is forced to wait upon him hand and foot (the last laugh of the film's English-language title).

Murnau's reputation as one of the true innovators of the early film industry is due in no small measure to his use of the *entfesselte Kamera* (unchained camera) in his films. Although the camera had not been entirely motionless beforehand, this concept became associated with Murnau and his cameraman Karl Freund after the release of *The Last Laugh* because of the innovative solutions Murnau and his team found to various challenges presented to them by the narrative. Thus the camera was variously placed on the front of a bicycle (for the opening long take of travelling down the hotel lift and out of the hotel lobby), on an elaborate platform and pulley/cable contraption (for the representation of sound flying out of the bell of a trumpet) as well as on what were by that time more conventional dollies and trolleys for a range of sequences. Murnau became the acknowledged master of this technique because he seems to have been the first to use movement as a narrative device, helping to develop the story. So great was the acclaim over the images in *The Last Laugh* that the film enabled Murnau to break into the lucrative American market – touring there himself in late 1925/early 1926 – and eventually to land a plum contract with Fox.

Towards the end of his career in Germany, Murnau returned to the portrayal of the *unheimlich* when he directed Ufa's flagship production of *Faust* (1927). Murnau had a startlingly clear vision of how to depict the story. Drawing upon a number of versions of the *Faust* legend, in the script by Hans Kyser, Mephisto (Emil Jannings) taunts the archangel Gabriel into a wager over the soul of the learned scientist Faust (Gösta Ekman). The ensuing battle sees Faust's home town ravaged by the plague. In desperation, Faust accepts Mephisto's offer of unlimited power and eternal youth. Only when he falls in love with the beautiful Gretchen (Camilla Horn) and loses her as a consequence of Mephisto's infernal meddling, does Faust renounce his pact with the devil and choose to burn with Gretchen at the stake. Some of the scenes demonstrate a total mastery of the medium in both composition and technical innovation. Murnau deploys his full range here – the use of *chiaroscuro* to heighten tension in the plague-ridden town, the dissolve shots which reveal rejuvenated versions of Faust and Mephisto, the exhilarating magic-carpet ride over the Altdorfer-inspired representation of the German countryside, and the post-production addition of rings of fire which surround Faust as he invokes the name of the devil (predating Lang's more celebrated use of the technique to film the Maria-robot transformation in *Metropolis*) all demonstrate Murnau's complete mastery of the medium of film.

In many ways *Faust* stands as an allegory of Weimar cinema, hinting at the price the filmmaker must pay to create such beautiful images. Frustrated by the demands of Ufa's studio system, which was already in decline, Murnau accepted an offer from Fox studios in Hollywood. By the time *Faust* premiered, Murnau had emigrated to America, and was never to return to Germany. Murnau directed three films for William Fox, including *Sunrise: A Song of Two Humans* in 1927, the only film ever to be granted an Academy Award 'For Unique Artistic Contribution'.[6] Ever restless, Murnau's last film was the independently produced *Tabu* (1930), shot in the Polynesian islands with the acclaimed documentary-maker Robert Flaherty.[7] Shortly before its premiere, however, he was fatally injured in a car accident near Santa Barbara in California. He died on 11 March 1931, aged 43, already viewed by many as one of the greatest directors of Weimar cinema, maybe even of the silent era. Charlie Chaplin is said to have described him as 'the best director Germany ever sent to Hollywood' (quoted in Prinzler 2003: 7), while Fritz Lang, who gave an oration at Murnau's graveside in Berlin, stated effusively 'film can be thankful that he has given it its very foundations ... His entire work was ballads in pictures' (quoted in Becker & Albrecht 1981: 110–11).

Nosferatu: eine Symphonie des Grauens

Murnau's 'Symphony of horror' *Nosferatu* stands as the pre-eminent expressionist horror film of the Weimar period. The conflation of a musical term in the film's subtitle with the supernatural motif epitomises Weimar's curious relationship with the *unheimlich*, for it suggests both approbation and fear of the unknown, as well as indicating the artistic portrayal of horror so common in German culture. This is most apparent when regarding the central figure, the vampire Count Orlok, otherwise known as Nosferatu.

The origins of the film are particularly illuminating. The co-scriptwriter and producer of the film, Albin Grau, had developed a fascination with the paranormal. He claimed to have heard stories of vampires whilst serving in the German army in eastern Europe during World War One, which inspired the film (see Eisner 1973: 109). The local name for such creatures was the 'nosferatu'. Grau founded his own production company, Prana Film, in 1921 with the ambitious aim of producing a programme of films dealing exclusively with supernatural themes, although *Nosferatu* was the only project which came to fruition. It was intended to be an adaptation of Bram Stoker's celebrated Gothic novel *Dracula* (1897), an example of the transnational nature of cinema even in its early days, but legal complications led Grau and fellow scriptwriter Henrik Galeen to adapt the screenplay in an attempt to disguise the film's origins.[8]

The storyline is very familiar to modern audiences: Thomas Hutter (Gustav von Wangenheim) works as an estate agent in the German town of Wisborg. As a result of his aspirations, perhaps, Hutter accepts a curious commission to travel to the Transylvanian residence of the mysterious Count Orlok,[9] who wishes to buy a property in Wisborg, directly opposite Hutter's house. His wife, Ellen (Greta Schröder) experiences dark premonitions and begs her husband not to go. Upon reaching Orlok's homeland, far in the East, strange events occur. The locals tell of evil legends, and wolves prowl the nighttime landscape. The mood of foreboding increases when Hutter is conveyed to Orlok's castle on a supernatural carriage journey through an eerie wood. It transpires that the Count is in fact a vampire, and Hutter falls victim to his demonic attentions. Worse still, when Orlok – the dreadful Nosferatu – glimpses a portrait of Ellen, he sets off to Wisborg, enthralled by her beauty. Hutter races after him to try to prevent the calamity which threatens.

Wherever Nosferatu goes, pestilence and disaster follow: the crew of his ship all die, and plague ravages Wisborg upon his arrival. Ellen in the meantime anticipates Nosferatu's arrival, and appreciates that only by keeping him in her bedroom until dawn can the town be saved. Hutter is powerless to prevent the tragedy unfolding. Ellen, now in Nosferatu's thrall, invites the monster into her bedroom. He enters her chamber, claiming his transfixed victim, and sates himself upon her blood all night long. Only as the cock crows does Nosferatu realise his folly in lingering too long, and disappears in a puff of smoke at dawn: Wisborg is safe.

Contemporary audiences and critics alike were reportedly gripped by the film. A sophisticated publicity campaign had preceded the film's launch, including rumours (no doubt initiated by the studio) that Schreck was a real vampire. And then the premiere itself, on 4 March 1922 at the Berlin Zoological Gardens, was followed by a lavish costume party. Critics were suitably impressed: 'an interesting (if not to say sensational) work', declared one (see Prinzler 2003: 130). The noted Hungarian film critic and theorist Béla Balázs went as far as to assure his readers: 'The images were all taken from nature. But a frosty breath of wind from beyond the grave blew through them all' (ibid.). Later, Lotte Eisner recognised how the sense of fear and foreboding in the film had been enhanced by the unusual techniques employed by Murnau during the shooting:

> Murnau created an atmosphere of horror by a forward movement of the actors towards the camera. The hideous form of the vampire approaches with exasperating slowness, moving from the extreme depth of one shot towards another in which he suddenly becomes enormous. Murnau had a complete grasp of the visual power that can be won from editing, and the virtuosity with which he directs this succession of shots has real genius. (1969: 102–3)

Indeed, many of the visual tricks, as well as some apparently conventional *mise-en-scène* lend the film a modernity which can surprise audiences today. In the scene where Hutter first encounters Nosferatu, for instance, the coach in which he is conveyed travels at abnormal speed through a forest of brilliantly white trees. This was achieved by cranking the camera at half the standard speed, then using a negative image of the scene in the finished film in order to unsettle the viewer. The carriage itself was painted white for the shoot, so that in a negative print it would appear black, as the audience might expect, against the eerie white backdrop of the forest. Stop-motion, too, is employed to show the canvas cover of the ship's hold rolling back by unseen agency when the vampire emerges from the bowels of the ship to terrorise Wisborg.

It is easy to see why the film is still a staple of expressionist film festivals today and is celebrated as one of the most important establishing works of the horror genre. Max Schreck's gestures, costume and make-up are directly inherited from the expressionist stage,[10] but this is purely a tool to enhance the uneasy, oppressive mood of the film through the portrayal of the Dracula character, since other characters' acting styles are largely conventional for the day. Lighting plays a key role, unsurprisingly, with many scenes being shot in a half-light which renders the edge of the frame almost totally black, but this again is perhaps to be expected of a film which is centred upon a hideous creature of the dark. Where *Nosferatu* comes into its own as an expressionist film is in its setting: although on the surface everything seems a realistic portrayal of the protagonists' world, in fact much is manipulated to underscore the supernatural element central to the plot. Even scenes which do not contain an ostensibly supernatural component, such as the views of landscapes, add to the sense of the uncanny here. Murnau had already been acknowledged as a director with a keen eye for the filmed landscape; contemporary reviews of his films frequently attest to this, even when the reviewer was perhaps otherwise unimpressed by the film as a whole. What is significant, though, is how such images enhance the sense of the *unheimlich* throughout the film: the mountains glower with an ethereal light which makes it difficult to place the time of day. Images of wooded slopes and rocky peaks are frequently intercut with shots of the main action to draw clear parallels between landscape and story. 'As always,' wrote Eisner in her monograph of this director, 'Murnau found visual means of suggesting unreality' (1973: 118).

Of great significance is the use of the arch, and of frames, in Murnau's *mise-en-scène*, particularly when combined with *chiaroscuro* lighting effects. When Hutter arrives at the castle, the sequence of him meeting Orlok is framed by the multi-layered arches of the castle keep. This signifies the location where Hutter's fate is sealed in a series of shots which reinforce the inevitability of the young couple's doom, revealing that they are trapped in much the same way as the fly offered to the Venus fly trap in the sequence featuring Professor Bulwer. Window frames, too, enhance subjectivity in the film, either cutting across the faces of the protagonists to act as imprisoning bars or to impede a view of one of the characters. They force the audience to share the point of view of the protagonists, often concealing as much as they reveal. The window (and its frame) becomes

Into the monster's lair: Hutter arrives at Count Orlok's castle

especially significant in the relationship between Ellen and Nosferatu, evidence of what David Robinson calls 'Murnau's uncompromisingly individual approach to Expressionism' (1973: 95). Firstly, when Orlok has reached Wisborg and the plague is claiming its dead, the viewer shares the point of view of Ellen when she looks out of her window at the pall bearers carrying the coffins to internment. Here, the cross-pattern of the frame hinders her (and our own) view of the townspeople below, suggesting that she is already isolated from the rest of society by her decision to offer herself to the vampire for the sake of her husband. As she turns away from the street she is drawn to the book wherein she learns that she must sacrifice herself to counter the vampire's malevolence. Later we see the Count himself, having taken up residence in buildings opposite the Hutter household, waiting for Ellen to call him. He is filmed behind the window, hands wrapped around the strong horizontal and vertical bars which demonstrate that the vampire is as much a prisoner, as much a victim, as Ellen and the others. The shadow of one of the bars falls across his face, holding him captive until Ellen's gesture will liberate him. She has been lying restlessly on her bed when she becomes aware of Orlok's vigil. She grips her breast, supernaturally aware of the vampire's intent, before walking to the window. With a brief, tender glance at her husband, asleep in a

Sacrifice and
sensuality: Ellen
invites the nosferatu
to her bedroom

chair, she turns to the window. The moonlight filters through her diapha-
nous nightgown, revealing the body beneath which she is now prepared
to sacrifice, as she flings open the window, her arms outstretched in an
approximation of crucifixion. Immediately, Nosferatu begins the final leg
of his journey to her. This latent sense of foreboding is further reinforced
by Murnau's use of *chiaroscuro* shadows in the film. Here shadows quite
clearly enhance the narrative, as Nosferatu's enlarged shadow is famously
seen climbing the stairs to Ellen's room. As she shrinks back to her bed,
the shadow of his clawed hand reaches across her body and clenches her
breast in triumph: only then do we see the vampire himself, feeding on
the limp body of the victim. Thus *thanatos* (death) and *eros* (sexuality) –
both regarded as frightening to a society still bound by strict Wilhelminian
values – are united in an orgasmic sequence: as sunlight floods into the
room the next morning, Nosferatu, who has slept with his head on Ellen's
body, shrinks from the sun's rays then arches his back and disappears in
a wisp of smoke.

Much of the film's success lies in its multiple readings, many of which
play on the notion of a threat to ordered society, either from without or
from within. The former idea is perhaps the most apparent, with Nosferatu
presenting a very real threat to the Hutters and to the town where they

live. The war on the Eastern front had been particularly unforgiving (as it was to prove again in the Second World War) and had served to reinforce the long-standing belief that the lands to the East of Germany were a threat to the Germans' existence. Nosferatu, an Eastern Count who travels to Germany to claim Hutter's wife, and who brings death and pestilence with him, conforms perfectly to these racial stereotypes, thus enhancing the thrill of fear generated by the film's images. When Nosferatu loads his earth-filled coffins for the journey westwards, and when the crew of the *Empusa* die in turn aboard the rat-infested ship, the audience shudders in unspoken acknowledgement of this xenophobia. For John Sandford, Count Orlok's ratlike appearance reinforces the sense of society overrun, citing the rat-infested ship which bears the vampire to Germany: 'Rats, and the plague that they bring with them, are, historically and in folk-memory, not native to northern Europe, but an invasive, "foreign" force from the East' (1995: 318). This association of rats, pestilence and invasion from the East, as well as Nosferatu's rat-like teeth and long fingernails, draws upon long-standing anti-Semitic prejudice, even before the Nazis began their concerted campaign against the Jews.[11]

Then there is the threat from within, which in this case centres on Hutter's wife. It should be noted that Weimar Germany was a society of rapid change, with the values of Wilhelminian Germany fighting a rear-guard action against the progressive, amoral values of the new, decadent order. Ellen is portrayed as a chaste, morally upright middle-class young woman, for whom marriage has little to do with love or fulfilment. She is very much the plaything of Hutter and the patriarchal society within which her repressed self is trapped, much as the ball she dangles before the kitten is used to tease and taunt the creature. Almost from the outset Ellen exhibits a supernatural understanding of the events which are unfolding at the count's castle. Here, again, Murnau's careful *mise-en-scène* suggests that, however much concern Ellen may have for her husband, in reality she is fascinated by the menace and virility of Nosferatu. Eyeline matches link the young bride with the vampire even when they are separated by great distances, and once Orlok has begun his voyage to Wisborg it is significant that Ellen goes to wait beside the sea, even though her husband is clearly travelling to her 'rescue' by land. In the scene where Ellen, dressed in black, waits among the dunes, the intertitles state only that she is 'pining for her beloved', without revealing the identity of the lover she awaits. As she

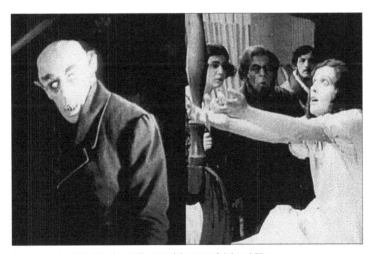

Supernatural connection: the eyeline match between Orlok and Ellen

sits and gazes out to sea, surrounded by the simple crosses of a sailors' graveyard, the sense of premonition, which has been present throughout, reaches new levels. It would seem that she is torn, subconsciously at least, between a sense of duty to her husband and the promise of fulfilment offered by the Count. As the film proceeds towards its dreadful conclusion, it becomes clear that the drive for personal sexual satisfaction prevails over the restrictions of societal mores. The restless sea (a favourite image of Murnau's and one which establishes a now-familiar trope in cinema) speaks figuratively of the complex undercurrents of desire and repression which torment the young woman. Thus, when Ellen lumbers to the window (her gait recalling that other somnambulist, Cesare, who is in Caligari's thrall), it is clear that she is already under the spell of the vampire: her shiver as she throws open the window is not simply due to the chill night air, but also highlights the frisson of anticipation with which she awaits her liberation. Although we might now see Nosferatu as the subconscious alter-ego of the sexually-repressed Hutter, in much the same way as the student of Prague was haunted by his double, the concept of a threat to the balance of society is startlingly clear.

Nosferatu has influenced successive generations of filmmakers, and Max Schreck's vampire has inspired many screen monsters. Indeed, there have been a number of screen tributes to Murnau's creation, including Werner Herzog's compelling remake *Nosferatu: Phantom der Nacht* (*Nosferatu: Phantom of the Night*, 1979). Then American author Jim Shepard published a semi-fictitious biographical novel about Murnau, entitled *Nosferatu in Love* (1998). This follows the director's career utilising a careful blend of established fact and creative fiction, including a fictitious diary of the shooting of *Nosferatu* itself. One entry reads: 'We look for the fantastic within ourselves' (1998: 102), Shepard suggesting an autobiographical, psychological impulse to Murnau's films of imperilled lovers. Later, E. Elias Merhige's film *Shadow of the Vampire* (2000) plays on the rumours of Max Schreck's vampirism to produce an amusing homage to Murnau's masterpiece, where the director (played by John Malkovich) offers Schreck (Willem Dafoe) the lives of minor crew members to sate his bloodlust, with the promise of Greta Schröder as his great reward at the end of shooting.

In an essay written by Murnau in 1928 he outlined the principles which underpinned his approach to filmmaking. As one of the true pioneers of the Weimar period he brought a painter's eye and a technician's understanding of the new medium which produced some of the freshest and most beautiful films of the era. 'Real art is simple', he began,

> but simplicity requires the greatest art. The camera is the director's sketching pencil. It should be as mobile as possible to catch every passing mood, and it is important that the mechanics of the cinema should not be interposed between the spectator and the picture. ... Everything is subordinated to my picture[s]. (2004: 68)

In the case of *Nosferatu*, Murnau took a simple scenario and, thanks to cinematic innovation and the subtle use of expressionist devices, greatly enhanced the sense of a supernatural threat. But the success of the film lies in its ability to subvert the medium to the story, thus ensuring that the chilling images of the vampire Nosferatu abide and chill audiences even today. *Nosferatu: A Symphony of Horror* thus stands for many at the pinnacle of Weimar cinema, with its perfect blend of story and technique. The notion of threat, of demons which can be seen as both an external and an internal danger, and the underlying sense of the *unheimlich* which pervades virtually every frame of the film have guaranteed that this early horror film has remained in the canon of great Weimar cinema ever since.

If Dr Caligari was Kracauer's prototype for Hitler and the hypnotic power he wielded over the German people, then we should perhaps develop his approach still further and acknowledge that the fear engendered in audiences by the vampire Nosferatu surely prefigures the terror of the National Socialists' victims a few years later. Thus the film gains added poignancy for the modern viewer since the vampire represents both the anti-Semitic fear of the Jewish/Eastern threat, as well as the sinister terror of the Nazis, at one and the same time. More apposite is the realisation that in the dreadful gaze of Count Orlok, Weimar audiences were both thrilled and repelled in equal measure, and along with the film's commercial success, in producing *Nosferatu* the young film industry took a huge step towards artistic legitimacy.

4   IMAGES OF THE PAST, VISIONS OF THE FUTURE: FRITZ LANG'S *DIE NIBELUNGEN* AND *METROPOLIS*

At the outset of the Weimar period, Germany was a country in disarray. Not only had the population suffered tremendous privations in the final months of World War One but they had done so still believing the claims of the German High Command that victory was imminent. The subsequent capitulation, followed on 9 November 1918 by the abdication of Prince Max von Baden, left the population reeling as the stark reality of their situation sank in. Soon disaffected members of the armed forces were in open revolt on the streets, left-wing alliances were declaring the formation of *Räterepubliken* (Communist ruling councils) in many of the major cities and Germany rapidly descended into chaos.

Then, when it seemed as if matters could hardly get any worse, the victorious Allies forced Germany's new political representatives to sign the Versailles Treaty, on 28 June 1919. Instead of demonstrating sympathy for the plight of the defeated nation, or proposing a package of measures to help the crippled infrastructure of the country to get back on its feet, the Allies (led by France and the new Soviet Union, whose countries had suffered terribly through German aggression) understandably insisted on swingeing reparations. The terms of the treaty included the transfer of large areas of German territory to the victors (notably the region of the Ruhr to French control and parts of Prussia to Poland and the Soviet Union), financial reparations to offset the loss of industrial capacity, and the reduction of the German armed forces to token levels only. If Germany was already on its knees in the winter of 1918, by the time the Weimar government had agreed to the terms of Versailles the country was at its lowest ebb.

Escapism in the cinema: Lubitsch and the past

Apart from the documentary films of everyday life (which had been part of cinemagoing from its very outset),[1] the narrative film quickly established itself as a staple of the main programme in cinemas throughout the country. The period of 1918–19, which Kracauer summed up with the phrase 'the shock of freedom' (1947: 43), saw so-called *Aufklärungsfilme* ('enlightenment films')[2] competing with the simple escapism of detective films, exotic adventures and historical epics. Ufa's chief executive in the early years quickly recognised the commercial potential of the historical film, exploiting the early star potential of the likes of Pola Negri and Emil Jannings in settings which were safely removed from the tribulations of daily life in postwar Germany. One director who well understood how to exploit this need for escapism was Ernst Lubitsch, who had begun his filmmaking career in the years before World War One. Between 1918 and 1922 he released several historical films, shot on a truly epic scale, which were massive successes both at home and (crucially at the time) abroad. Of these, *Madame Dubarry* (*Passion*, 1919) and *Anne Boleyn* (*Deception*, 1920) were the greatest successes, set in Revolutionary France and six-teenth-century England respectively and featuring large crowd scenes with many hundreds of hungry soldiers still looking for employment – and food – in the aftermath of their demobilisation (see Elsaesser 2000a: 195ff). Lubitsch succeeded in combining an eye for grand spectacle with a lighter, comedic vein, giving rise to the notion of the 'Lubitsch touch' (see Hake 2002: 33–4), which lent his films an international appeal. This quickly resulted in a lucrative offer from Hollywood, which Lubitsch accepted after directing his last German film *Das Weib des Pharao* (*The Wife of Pharaoh*) in 1922. Never part of the expressionist movement in Weimar, Lubitsch went on to enjoy a notable career in the United States, including several Academy Award nominations and an honorary Academy Award in 1947 for his contribution to the motion picture industry.

Escapism in the cinema: science fiction

A different response to the troubles of the day was only gradually to be observed in Weimar's cinemas: science fiction. As a literary genre science fiction had enjoyed a certain status in pre-war Germany, thanks to the long-standing popularity of authors such as Jules Verne (*Voyage to the Centre of the Earth*, 1864; *From the Earth to the Moon*, 1865) and H. G. Wells (*War of the Worlds*, 1898). In the earliest days of cinema, some of these literary works were dramatised by pioneering filmmakers, such as Georges Méliès' *Le voyage dans le lune* (*A Trip to the Moon*, 1902), but the genre struggled to establish itself in the first postwar years.[3] Perhaps the situation on the ground was simply too awful to imagine any kind of future. Yet a certain appeal remained, largely centring on the modernist appeal of the USA, with its flourishing automobile industry and its skyscraper-dominated cities. It is no surprise, perhaps that the young boy who features in Fritz Lang's science fiction film *The Woman in the Moon* reads American science fiction comics and dreams of travelling to space. Whereas America with its reputation for modernism could be comfortably associated with space travel, and by extension, science fiction, this was not the case in a still-reactionary Germany of the postwar period. National identity, the collective self-esteem, was simply too battered at this stage to escape into the future. Even the expressionists who continued to work after the War did not translate their modernist ideas into predictions of the future, so uncertain were the times through which they were living. In the end, it took an Austrian filmmaker to address the issue of German national identity through films which both interpreted the past and predicted the future in equal measure.

Fritz Lang

Born on 5 December 1890 in Vienna, Friedrich Christian Anton Lang was the second son to Anton and Paula Lang, an upper middle-class couple (he non-practising Catholic, she liberal Jewish) in the boom years of the Austrian *fin de siècle* era. The two boys (his elder brother had been born six years earlier) enjoyed a rather liberal upbringing which included regular family trips to the theatre and evenings of poetry and music appreciation in the family home. After a privileged school education, Lang half-heartedly pursued university courses in art and art history. He then succumbed to the café culture of Vienna and the performing arts scene in the Austrian capital, which greatly disappointed his father. In 1910 Lang left Vienna, following arguments with his father, to begin a period of itinerant travelling. His journeys reputedly took him to Brussels, Paris and even India and the Far East before Lang chose to settle in Paris in 1913.

This somewhat idyllic period in his life was cut short by World War One. It seems that Lang narrowly avoided internment by the French authorities before making his way to Vienna, where he volunteered for active duty in January 1915. Army records show that as a mounted artillery observer he often faced grave danger, several times having horses killed beneath him, to produce sketches of the enemy's positions. More than once he suffered serious wounds which resulted in promotion, official recognition of his bravery (including Austria's highest military honour, the *Karl Truppenkreuz*) and required that Lang wear an eyepatch or monocle over his damaged eye.

During periods of leave and convalescence back in Vienna, Lang became attracted to the film industry and began to write film treatments and scripts. The already-prominent producer and director Joe May (see chapter 6) contracted Lang to provide him with a number of stories, several of which were filmed by May himself, although Lang was unhappy at the lack of recognition he was getting. Soon after Lang was introduced to Erich Pommer, who immediately arranged for the young man's permanent transfer out of the army and whisked him to Berlin, to work in the Decla-Bioscop studio.[4] The young man's first directorial opportunity came when he negotiated with Pommer to film his own script, *Halbblut* (*Half Blood*), which premiered in April 1919 to general acclaim.

Recognition quickly followed. Lang displayed a remarkable talent for gripping storylines, no doubt fired by a childhood reading German novelist Karl May's tales of Cowboys and Indians and other stories of adventure and exoticism.[5] To this he added a talented eye for seemingly placing the audience right in the midst of the action. With the commercial success of the two-parter *Spinnen* (*Spiders*, 1919/20), critics acknowledged a new talent in the world of German cinema.

Then in 1920 Lang met the talented author, actress and scriptwriter Thea von Harbou. Both were married at the time but they soon embarked on an affair; their professional collaboration was phenomenally productive. On 7 October 1921 the first Lang/von Harbou collaboration *Der müde Tod* (*Destiny*) premiered in Berlin and seemed to cement Lang's reputation as a talented director. Perhaps some of its success was down to the flamboyant stories about Lang and his scriptwriter lover, gleefully reported by the film press; none more so than the fact that Lang's wife allegedly shot herself after finding the couple *in flagrante* at the Lang home. Although subsequent investigations concluded that the death was indeed suicide, rumours persisted that Lang had in fact shot his wife himself and staged her suicide. Lang eventually married von Harbou on 26 August 1922, but the passion between the two did not last and they divorced eleven years later when Lang elected to flee the regime.

In the meantime, Lang and von Harbou enjoyed runaway success. *Destiny* was followed by one of Lang's great films, *Dr Mabuse, der Spieler* (*Dr Mabuse, the Gambler*, 1922) the four-hour tale of a criminal master-mind, with the eponymous gangster played by von Harbou's ex-husband, Rudolf Klein-Rogge, in the first of several similar roles he played for Lang. Subtitled 'A Picture of our Times', Mabuse's manipulations of the political and economic situation virtually implied that Germany's woes could be attributed to the manipulations of such a criminal, and the film's finale – depicting the criminal gang holed up in a house, exchanging gunfire with troops and armed police – must have struck a nerve with the audience.

Lang and von Harbou went from strength to strength, producing the epics *Nibelungen* and *Metropolis* during the middle, stable years of the Weimar Republic: films shot on a grand scale to which we shall return shortly. By the end of the 1920s Lang was at the height of his creative powers. The thriller *Spione* (*Spies*, 1928) saw Klein-Rogge reprise his role as a criminal mastermind, while *The Woman in the Moon* utilised all of Ufa's resources to create a true science fiction film, with fabulous models built to stage the launch sequence,[6] and elaborate effects shots to create the illusion of weightlessness, for instance. Finally, in 1931, Lang made a hugely successful foray into the world of sound cinema (indeed, he is one of the very few directors of the Weimar cinema to do so with any real success), releasing his highly-acclaimed film about the serial murderer Hans Beckert, *M*, starring Peter Lorre. Lang took sound to be an extension of his repertoire, using both sound (most famously the murderer's whistling leitmotif) and – critically – the absence of sound, to signal moods and enhance tension in the narrative.

Lang's insistence on total control of the image, and his use of *chiaro-scuro* effects of light and shadow in his films, coupled with a *mise-en-scène* which frequently seeks to reveal a character's inner workings, all serve to suggest that he was an expressionist filmmaker very much in the mould of Wiene or Murnau. But Lang was a complex character, to say the least, and it is worth noting the response of his Mabuse character when asked about the impact of Expressionism on German society: 'Expressionism? It's just a game. Everything is a game nowadays.'

Lang's German career was cut short by the rise of the Nazis. Although many of his autobiographical anecdotes – such as stories of interviews with Goebbels, and hurried train journeys into exile – should be viewed with some circumspection, by 1934 he had begun a career in Hollywood. Best-known for his thrillers suffused with what became his trademark *noir* style, he enjoyed notable success with, amongst others, his debut film in America, *Fury* (1936), the anti-Nazi *Hangmen Also Die* (1943) and *Scarlet Street* (1945). Becoming more and more of a recluse in his later years, nearly blind and eventually bedridden, Lang died after suffering a stroke on the morning of 2 August 1976, in his home in Hollywood.

Images of the Past: Die Nibelungen

Lang was eternally grateful to his adopted homeland Germany and wanted to give something back to a nation which was still suffering from what he perceived to be a deep sense of loss after the war. Years later he recalled the process by which he had come to the filming of *Die Nibelungen*:

> I wanted to show that Germany was searching for an ideal in her past, even during the horrible time after the First World War in which the picture was made. To counteract the pessimistic spirit of the time, I wanted to film the great legend of Siegfried so that Germany could draw inspiration from her epic past. (Quoted in McGilligan 1997: 104)

In typical fashion for the German film industry in the 1920s, which preferred the 'director-unit' system (see Elsaesser 2000: 27), Lang proceeded with his established team of artists and technicians: set designer Robert Herlth, cameraman Eugen Schüfftan and art directors Otto Hunte, Karl Vollbrecht and Erich Kettelhut. All members were involved in the pre-production planning of the film and were consulted throughout shooting. As Kettelhut later recalled, 'every set and every detail, every position in every one of an actor's movements, was discussed in detail and the pros and cons of every opinion thoroughly analysed … No wonder the production meetings took almost three months' (quoted in McGilligan 1997: 95).

The hero Siegfried in
Ufa's primeval forest

The first part of the *Nibelungen* story, *Siegfrieds Tod* (*Siegfried's Death*, 1924), tells of how the Aryan hero Siegfried (Paul Richter) resolves to win the hand of the beautiful Kriemhild (Margarete Schoen) of the Burgundians. He defeats the dragon Fafnar and is rendered invincible by bathing in the dragon's blood. Only one spot, inadvertently covered by a falling leaf as he bathes, remains unprotected. Siegfried later defeats the dwarf Alberich, who offers him a magic veil granting him the ability to make himself invisible. He claims the treasure of the Nibelungs and arrives at the court of King Günther (Theodor Loos) to win Kriemhild as his bride.

Günther's champion Hagen (Hans Adalbert Schlettow), however, resents Siegfried's favourable standing in the court and works with Günther's wife Brunhild (Hanna Ralph) to bring about the hero's downfall. On a hunt, Hagen ambushes Siegfried and pierces his vulnerable shoulder with a spear.[7] When the hero's body is carried back to court, Kriemhild swears vengeance on her husband's killers.

In the second part of the saga, *Kriemhilds Rache* (*Kriemhild's Revenge*, also released 1924), Kriemhild agrees to marry Attila, King of the Huns (another key role for Rudolf Klein-Rogge). She regards this marriage as no more than an opportunity to exact her revenge on Hagen, and her brother

King Günther. When Kriemhild bears Attila a son, she slyly suggests that her brother be invited to attend a celebratory feast. Once the Burgundian entourage have arrived, Kriemhild provokes a confrontation which results in Attila's heir being murdered by Hagen. Attila withdraws from court, numbed by grief, leaving the way free for Kriemhild to encourage her clansmen to attack the Burgundians. Coldly, Kriemhild orders the burning of the hall, until Günther and Hagen, the only survivors, stagger out of the fire. Both men expect and receive no quarter, with Hagen dying by Siegfried's sword, wielded by Kriemhild herself. Yet even as her task is complete, the vengeful widow collapses to the ground, her all-consuming rage having exhausted her, and she dies. Attila announces that she will be buried alongside Siegfried, and the tale closes.

Lang drew upon his art training in these films, taking inspiration from paintings by the likes of Frank von Stuck, Gustav Klimt and Caspar David Friedrich in individual scenes. The fantastically-designed sets with their heavily stylised *mise-en-scène*, the expressionist use of stark contrast in key scenes and the almost brutal geometry of the décor in the Burgundian court are ample evidence of Lang's unerring knack for producing a film guaranteed to appeal to the broadest possible audience. To this artistic sensibility Lang added innovative cinematography to turn the scenes in his imagination into images onscreen. Examples include the use of double exposure (with the film in the camera, cranked back by hand) to reproduce the movements of the invisible hero as he helps King Günther defeat Brunhilde, and of course the enormous animated dragon, which required a sizable crew of stage hands to operate, and even belched real smoke and fire!

Filming took a staggering nine months, almost unheard of at a time when many directors were still producing several films in a single year, and German film production in total ran to several hundred annually.[8] Eisner recalls how this lengthy shoot at least had the advantage that real snow could be used on the set of the glade where Siegfried is betrayed (1976: 75). Other accounts show Lang presiding over the external shots of the Huns riding across the steppes (filmed on Berlin's Rehbergen hills close to the Babelsberg studios), sitting astride a white horse, resplendent in his jodhpurs and monocle, and directing proceedings by means of a large megaphone (see McGilligan 1997: 99). The climax of the shooting, and of the film, came in January 1924 when the final apocalyptic scene of the doom of the Burgundians in Attila's hall was filmed in a specially-converted factory in Spandau. Lang, with his typical mixture of control-freakery and love of danger, insisted on firing the first flaming arrow to commence the pyrotechnic spectacular.

In *Die Nibelungen* Lang fully exploits the potential of cinema to depict a mythical world in transition. Expressionist techniques can be seen in the shooting of many scenes: from the murky primeval forest where Siegfried begins his quest, to the strictly geometric and regimented court of Burgundy, and then on to the earthy, organic chaos of the realm of the Huns, the film depicts a world struggling to assert itself against the tides of history. Lang seamlessly weaves together the ancient text with the most advanced tricks of his young trade to show how the heroes – and villains – of this epic national tale strive to establish themselves against the seemingly implacable forces of destiny, or, as Tom Gunning describes it, the Destiny-machine. For Gunning, every element in this film (as indeed in Lang's others) is subverted to this principle:

> In this film the uncanny quality comes from an absolute elimina-
> tion of the contingent, natural or accidental, in favour of the heavily
> designed, calculated and predetermined, so that even the fall of
> a leaf [when Siegfried bathes in the dragon's blood] can set the
> Destiny-machine in motion. (2000: 40)

Even within the diegetic progress of the film, action is related both as oral tradition (such as stories related to courtiers and songs sung by courtly bards), and also as a self-referential cinematic experience (such as when Alberich 'projects' images of the hidden Nibelung treasure onto a cave wall). In this way Lang reminds his audience that this story of bravery and treachery carries a message as relevant to the 1920s as any other era. When the bard Volker sings of Siegfried's acts of heroism against the dragon, it is telling that the Burgundian court sits transfixed, almost literally petrified just as the dwarfs had been, whilst supporting the hoard of treasure liber-ated by Siegfried. Only Kriemhild, who is to be the prime figure over the course of the two films – the one who forges the destiny path which all the others will follow, willingly or otherwise – seems able to break free of the song's spell as she presents the bard with the gift of a cloak. Nevertheless her love for the hero, of whom she has heard only vicariously, is clear.

When Siegfried arrives at the court of Worms, the centre of the film's civilised world, it seems inconceivable that the film will end in the ashes of Attila's court, with death and destruction wrought upon every character, yet the signs are there from the very beginning. He is accompanied by an honour guard every bit as artfully placed as the columns and windows of the set itself. It seems that he has left the chaotic, natural but dangerous and uncivilised world of the Germanic forest far behind. Yet almost as soon as he reaches the dais where King Günther sits, Hagen's instant dislike of the hero quickly reveals that the world of civilised behaviour is only a thin veneer. Governed by his emotions, Hagen's immediate antipathy towards Siegfried is the root of all the sorrow to come. King Günther, on the other hand, places his faith in the law of courtly behaviour through which, so he believes, such atavistic emotions as Hagen's are kept in check, if not entirely banished. In the kingdom of the Huns, too, Attila fervently believes that 'in the desert where I was born there is but one thing sacred, the guest'.

All of this is prefigured artfully in the set design and *mise-en-scène* of Lang's film. In the ancient forests of the opening sequences, smoke and mist drift among the trees, representing the living force of the earth seeping through and moving amongst those who live there. The court of King Günther is apparently above this, literally as well as figuratively, since images of the castle upon the rocks are bathed in an almost preternatural light. But a primitive miasma can still be observed at key moments, seeping into the civilised world: the incense burning in the cathedral as Siegfried and Kriemhild marry; or the smoke from the hearths of Brunhild's chambers, and later in Attila's palace; the fierce wind which whips mist across the bridge when Siegfried's body is carried back to the palace. Similarly, the archways at the entrance to the courts of Günther and Attila recall the caves where Siegfried once lived with mythical folk, and Kriemhild descends to subterranean caves to incite the Huns to act out her desire for revenge on the Burgundian soldiers attending her son's feast.

This process of the reinforcement of plot through design is nowhere more clear than at the moment of Siegfried's betrayal. The spring where the hero is ambushed is a triumph of Weimar cinema's approach to studio-based filming, where artificial slopes are bedecked with carefully planted flowers and birch trees. The trees surround the spring, and as Siegfried cups water in his hand they create a wonderful visual backdrop, their

Treachery in paradise
as Siegfried dies at
the hands of Hagen

straight white trunks echoing the geometry of the Burgundian court. These formal verticals are then destroyed when Hagen throws the hefty spear, its girth almost as great as the birches, whose line breaks across the verticals of the trees at an acute angle. Thus the act of treachery is visually and figuratively reinforced by the destruction of the geometry which stands for civilised behaviour, once governed by morality and the law but now cast aside by baser human emotions. Hagen's spear has literally destroyed the equilibrium of the Burgundian (for which read civilised) world, and, within the narrative at least, nothing will ever be the same again.

Thus, it transpires, the world of civilisation is not so far removed from the realm of fantasy and myth which it has replaced. When Kriemhild stands in the courtyard of Attila's palace and watches her kinsmen perish with barely a flicker of remorse, she is asked by a retainer 'Are you not human, Lady Kriemhild?' to which she replies stonily 'No, I died when Siegfried died.' Thus, in an echo of one of the commonest elements of the expressionist films, the film becomes a kind of dream, an oneiric song of praise to *thanatos* (the classical Greek conception of death), which tells the audience that law and honour, duty and civilisation are merely superficial overlays concealing the more elemental emotions of love and hatred. Lang and von Harbou here craft a marvellous, sweeping tale of human emotions, on an epic scale, which at the same time was designed to unite the German nation after the shattering experience of the World War One. At the film's premiere on 14 February 1924 Chancellor Gustav Stresemann 'expressed the hope that the Nibelungen film would unite the German people and build a bridge to other nations', while the same day Lang and von Harbou laid a wreath at the grave of Frederick the Great (see Kaes 2002: 65), celebrated in common memory as Germany's finest leader. Even associations with Nazism, which plagued the film for a number of years, cannot tarnish the visual and technical brilliance of Lang's epic.[9]

Patrick McGilligan enthuses: 'Seen today, *Die Nibelungen* remains one of the breathtaking wonders of the silent screen' (1997: 101). In a comment which reflects the kind of language seen in the early expressionist manifestos, he goes on to expand on his assertion: 'Lang was never more in command of his flair for drama and sensation on a panoramic scale. Every scene is inventively dappled with sparkle and haze, smoke and fire, gusts of wind, reflection in water and mirrors, and the constant interplay of shadow and lights' (ibid.).

Images of the Future: Metropolis

In *Die Nibelungen*, Lang explained, 'I was dealing with Germany's legendary heritage [whereas] in *Metropolis*, I was looking at Germany in the future' (quoted in McGilligan 1997: 104). Thus the emphasis switches from past to future, as Gunning suggests, recognising the essentially timeless nature of both films: 'The purported era of the two films actually serve the same end ... removing the stories from any direct reference to the contemporary environment ... and allowing them to take place in an entirely constructed and symbolic environment' (2000: 34–5). With Lang's reputation, and the positive response to *Die Nibelungen*, success was surely guaranteed and Ufa were prepared to invest vast sums of money in the project.

But Gunning recognises the difficulties associated with the film, acknowledging: '*Metropolis* remains the albatross around Lang's neck' (2000: 52), and he is not alone in this appraisal. In *Metropolis,* Ufa handed Lang its flagship film of the later Weimar period, pouring vast quantities of money into the production in the vain hope that the tale would enhance Ufa's position in the lucrative US market. The fact that so much was riding on the success of the film possibly explains its convoluted developments in the immediate aftermath of its release and ever since.

The film opens on a world of stark contrasts. While the faceless, nameless workers march to their shifts, serving insatiable machinery in the bowels of the city, the rich and the powerful frolic in pleasure parks literally high above their heads. This vertical separation is disrupted, however, when Maria (Brigitte Helm) brings a group of workers' children to the Eternal Gardens where Freder (Gustav Fröhlich) is cavorting with young women of his class. Freder is instantly captivated by the vision of Maria's beauty. He follows her down to the underground city and there witnesses for the first time in his sheltered life the true horrors of life as a worker. In a vision he sees the workers literally fed into the mouth of the city's machinery, now transformed into a living beast, which then explodes, maiming workers indiscriminately.

Freder is horrified to discover that his father Joh Fredersen (played by Alfred Abel, a staple of early Weimar film) is not only aware of the conditions of the workers but approves of them. All he fears is that Maria's religious exhortations – she likens their city to the biblical Tower of Babel, which stood and fell as a symbol of man's hubris – will spread to the workers and result in revolution.

At Joh's request the scientist Rotwang (Rudolf Klein-Rogge again) kidnaps Maria and transforms her into a robot, ready to do the overlord's bidding. The robot-Maria sows discord amongst the workers and, using her flagrant sexuality, creates chaos amongst the wealthy classes. At the same time, parallel scenes make it quite clear that the biblical whore of Babylon has unleashed forces in the city that cannot easily be stopped. As the machines are smashed, hidden reservoirs burst and the underground city of the workers floods, threatening to drown their children who are trapped there. Only the intervention of Freder and the real Maria, who has been freed, saves the city from total destruction. Once order has been restored Maria encourages Freder to act as the mediator, helping the workers and Joh Fredersen to be reconciled in fulfilment of her prophecy: 'The mediator between the head and hands must be the heart.'

It seems incredible now that Lang should strike out in such a novel direction for this project, but essentially *Metropolis* was another episode in Lang's accounts of the heart of the German nation. Having examined the legends of an earlier era, constructing a past which consisted of myth, magic and heroism, the emphasis has moved to a future landscape upon which the shortcomings of the present could be projected as warning sirens. As such, Lang hit a nerve, for although the film was almost immediately accused of an over-complicated plot, and ran massively over-budget to stretch Ufa's resources virtually to breaking point, the imagery of *Metropolis* may well have appealed to a nation which had itself muddled through several years of chaos and confusion. That much of the imagery of *Metropolis* should have endured to this day is testimony to Lang's vision and creative energies.[10]

The genesis of the film appears as tortuous as its plot. The script, drawing on a wide range of sources (see Elsaesser 2000b) had been developed by Thea von Harbou from the summer of 1923. By 1924 meticulous pre-production meetings were held between Lang, von Harbou and various key members of the crew. Then, in October 1924, Lang embarked on a long promotional tour of the USA for Ufa, accompanied by Erich Pommer. Together they sailed on the *S.S. Deutschland* to attend the US premiere of *Die Nibelungen*. Lang recalled how he was captivated by the New York skyline which greeted him as he waited to come ashore. In later years he even went so far as to claim that this was the moment when he actually conceived of *Metropolis*, and although this cannot be the case, it seems clear that the American trip was a crucial experience for Lang as he prepared for this new project.

Shooting began on 22 May 1925, and lasted a staggering 310 days (as well as encompassing some 60 nights of shooting). Although many scenes were straightforward enough, it was the sequences where Lang envisaged his futuristic society which caused the greatest difficulties. A whole range of new special effects innovations had to be marshalled to the effort: from the slow wipes and dissolves used to show the robot's transformation and the morphing of Maria's facial features onto the robot's expressionless mask, to the stop-motion cityscapes with cars shooting along suspended freeways as aircraft circle above and below, many establishing shots took days (even weeks) to create, sometimes for the sake of a few seconds' screen time. Erich Kettelhut tells of one sequence where the film had to be exposed, in camera, over thirty times before the requisite image was captured (see Elsaesser 2000b: 25) and the effects editor Egon Schüfftan perfected a technique whereby live action was shot through a painted plate of glass to mix real images with forced perspective two-dimensional backdrops. In *Metropolis* this Schüfftan process, as it came to be known, was used to film the sequences of the city's machinery transformed into a monster, devouring the workforce amidst a hellish scene of fire and smoke. Despite such bold shots, however, from the very outset a great deal of criticism was aimed at the plot.

From the outset, *Metropolis* courted controversy and has frequently been the subject of revision and re-editing. After a long publicity campaign where 'expectations had been raised to fever pitch' (Elsaesser 2000b: 29) the film's premiere was held at the Ufa-Palast am Zoo in Berlin on 10 January 1927. Here the audience was shown a film of over 4000 metres length, lasting very nearly three hours. Reception was mixed, with warm applause for director and actors mixed with murmurings about an overly-complex narrative and unnecessary plot asides. By the time Ufa had presented it for US distribution, nervous executives had already ordered the film to be recut but it was then further shortened by Paramount who felt that anything over two hours was asking for trouble.[11] By the time the film debuted at the New York Rialto on 7 March, no more than three quarters of the original film remained and a number of intertitles had been amended. When Ufa hastily edited their version still further, before a scheduled re-release in the summer of 1927, it was clear that Lang's original film was all but lost. Ever since, film historians have striven to restore *Metropolis* to its original state.

Whatever the issues with the treatment of the film over the years, its status as a classic has been firmly established in recent decades. Amongst many interpretations, some critics read the film as a continuation of Lang's obsession with fate and destiny (see Gunning 2000), others prefer a reading which artfully combines Expressionism's fear of technology with the older fear of the sexually-aggressive woman (see Huyssen 1996), or a morality tale about existential angst and issues of identity (see Pike 2004). Finally, the film has been read as an allegory of the period in film history where old-world, reactionary Europe vies for supremacy against the new-world, modernist and – most irritatingly – *nouveau riche* America, and Hollywood in particular (see Minden 2000).

But in the context of this study, what proves most interesting is the way in which *Metropolis* serves as a mirror of its own time, with the science fiction setting having only a minimal bearing upon our reading of the film. ' ang glimpsed amongst the skyscrapers of New York a positive vision of ‾ope's future but the vision in *Metropolis* is far from utopian. Indeed, contemporary reviews complained that the film failed to offer much by way of predictions of a future lifestyle. While we see glimpses of a video-phone, and the architecture of the city itself implies a certain technological sophistication, airships still circle overhead and the dress of the protago-nists is rarely even avant-garde.[12]

What remains, then, if we strip away the science fiction tag which has been attached to *Metropolis*? The answer is still not obvious: possibly a biblical allegory of the workers patiently waiting for a Messiah to mediate between themselves and the eternal father; or a Marxist critique of capital-ist exploitation of the labour force, which requires a (presumably socialist) resolution to effect better labour relations; a warning that technology is a blessing only in part; or all – or indeed none – of the above? Thomas Elsaesser considers the film to be 'animated more by high-voltage floures-cence than Expressionism's dark demonic urges' (2000b: 7) but then sums up the apparently mutually exclusive strands of the film's plot by examin-ing the film against the backdrop of the society within which it emerged:

Metropolis's incoherence ... is a matter of perspective ... Despite its lack of realism, the film is something of a psychogram or fever-chart of the late 20s, which across its tale of technology run riot and industrial regimentation, is obsessed with rising tempera-tures, pressures coming to a head, bubbling liquids on the boil, imminent explosions and inundating floods: in short, it records all manner of forces welling up from the deep. (2000b: 16)

This concept of an expressionist-inspired 'psychogram' seems to serve well here, since another way to interpret *Metropolis* is as a presentation of dreams. Throughout the film, overt visions and dream sequences are mixed with rather more understated elements of longing and the gaze. This allows a pertinent question here, namely: whose point of view is represented in *Metropolis*? In many ways Freder can be regarded as the cinema-goer in Weimar Germany, Kracauer's archetypal emasculated citizen who has seen the horrors of the war, and its aftermath, and has then observed Germany descend into political chaos in the early years of the Weimar Republic. The fantasy played out in *Metropolis* then, one which Lang with his desire to give something to the German people would be drawn towards, is that the viewer may yet find the courage to restore order and effect the reconcilia-tion seen on the steps of the cathedral in the film's (somewhat mawkish)

The inventor Rotwang and his woman-machine Maria

closing scene. The leader figure, who tried to exert total control by making use of the robot-double of Maria has failed to retain that control, as has the mad-scientist Rotwang (who in a curious twist on the *Caligari* story finds that it is he who must attempt to escape across the rooftops with the girl, while his robot/somnambulist who turned against all her masters, is burned at the stake by the angry mob).

Yet another interpretation is revealed if we move away from Lang's fantasy/reality representations and look at the political persuasions of Thea von Harbou, who was a committed nationalist. In a pseudo-religious allegory, her script envisages an as yet unidentified messianic figure, mediating between labour and management, in a brand of political leadership which was precisely how National Socialism saw itself in the late 1920s. If Kracauer attacked what he called Lang's 'grand-style manner' (1947: 149), and accused him and von Harbou of creating a film 'rich in subterranean content that, like contraband, had crossed the borders of consciousness without being questioned' (1947: 163), then he did so precisely because it was all too easy to see how the Nazis appropriated this sense of mediation to their own aims. But Lang, in 1927 still a few years away from voluntary exile in the USA, appears to be warning the audience not to accept leadership at face-value. The sexual provocation of the robot-Maria turns (mostly male) heads in a way which Lang brilliantly depicts with his montage sequence of grossly-expanded eyes, in turn pointing to the potential of cinema to dazzle, to divert the attention. As Gunning rightly points out:

'Nothing changes at the end – Grot is a foreman and management snitch, Freder is the pampered son of the boss who claims to understand the workers after a single gruelling shift, Joh remains the boss despite his will-ingness to destroy the whole city rather than relinquish control over it to Maria' (2000: 78–9). Whilst *Die Nibelungen* showed that the strict geom-etry of the Burgundian court was little more than a hastily-applied veneer which still leaked the miasmic fog of atavistic jealousy and desire, Lang's futuristic vision of society merely rendered the façade of civilisation more visible. The city of Metropolis is built quite literally on inequality, on sub-terranean caverns which the favoured leaders do not care about and do not want to know about. Like Siegfried's blood, the floodwaters which erupt from beneath the city are a sign of the forces which lie concealed beneath the surface. Yet even when primitive, elemental forces are unleashed in Lang's films, the harsh reality is that change is very difficult to achieve and life reverts to the way it was.

In the case of Lang, we see a director who quickly appreciated the promise of cinema as a medium for subversive images and who was eager to exploit the potential of film as both an entertainment business and a torch-bearer for culture. He was unabashed in interviews when talking of his aims throughout his career to make films which not only entertained in the popular (and successful) sense but which also brought culture closer to the average cinema-goer, who was traditionally from the lower classes; if the appropriation of elements of expressionist *mise-en-scène* was a nec-essary part of this aim, then so be it. In an interview given at the time of the release of *Die Nibelungen* in 1924 he stated boldly, 'I may boast to have been one of those among the passionate pioneers for the development of film who have fought most fiercely for the claim that film is called upon to develop itself from a vapid entertainment industry to an artwork, and I may well say with pride and pleasure that I have succeeded in this through the splendid association with Erich Pommer, the chairman of the board of … Dekla-Bioskop-Ufa' (2004: 61).

By reanimating the legends of the past, as well as by positing images of the future, Lang fervently believed that he could make a contribution to the everyday lives of the men and women who walked the streets of Berlin and elsewhere in Weimar Germany. The fact that so many of his best scenes became associated with National Socialism in the aftermath of Hitler's ill-fated *Reich* is a terrible irony, but one which also galvanised

Lang to mobilise film in ever-more political terms during his second career in the United States. As a painter of the times which he experienced in Germany between 1918 and 1931, Lang was certainly one of Weimar's very best directors.

5   VIRGINS AND VAMPS: G. W. PABST'S *DIE BÜCHSE DER PANDORA*

One factor in the growth of the Weimar film industry was the commercial interests of the studios and the cinemas, both institutions understandably predicated on maximising profit from their investment in the product.[1] Although this growth might have been held back in the early years, when the reparations of the Versailles Treaty created conditions of soaring inflation, the middle years of the decade saw no such difficulties. The Dawes Plan, a package of financial measures designed to breathe life into Germany's floundering economy, finally stabilised the *Reichsmark* and as industry recovered so unemployment was brought under control. As a consequence, people had money in their pockets again and consumerism rose while the leisure industries boomed. Any lingering doubts about the success of the cinema, whether in commercial or economic terms, were brushed aside: both production and viewing figures soared.

It was not long before the film actors became commodities in their own right, and none more so than the women who dazzled audiences with their beauty and their glamour. Thus the double escape of film – of immersing oneself in the narrative, but also dreaming of stardom – became a crucial aspect of cinemagoing in the Republic.

Early stars and star potential

Weimar's very first film stars were the (mostly male) actors who had established their reputations on the stage. Thus Werner Krauss, Emil Jannings and Conrad Veidt, for example, had already enjoyed acclaim and respect in many stage plays and several early films by the time of Wiene's *Dr Caligari* or Lubitsch's *Passion*. Others, such as Alfred Abel or Rudolf Klein-Rogge had also established themselves as stalwarts of the Weimar film scene, giving rise to the new phenomenon of audience identification with familiar faces.

It is not the aim of this study to analyse the reasons behind stardom in Germany in the 1920s, but a number of issues are pertinent here and should be noted. In terms of exposure, for example, many of Weimar's stars appeared in dozens of films a year, ranging from cheap melodramas and simple comedies to thrilling spy yarns and attempts at art-house respectability. Secondly, and perhaps most crucially, the industry behind filmmaking thrived on hype – initially it was the films themselves which were heralded with expensive and imaginative advertising campaigns, but increasingly the names of the stars signed up to appear in the films enjoyed at least equal prominence in the studios' advertising campaigns. Indeed, by the end of the period in question, certain films were produced specifically to act as star vehicles, intended to capitalise on the appeal of a particular actor both at home and abroad.

It did not take long for the glamour of the female actors to eclipse that of their male counterparts. Some of the first women to become household names were Austrian-born Mia May,[2] or Lubitsch's leading ladies, Pola Negri, the lead in *Passion* and Henny Porten, who had starred in Lubitsch's *Deception*. Another to come to prominence in this period was Lya de Putti, who starred alongside Mia May in husband Joe May's *Das indische Grabmal* (*The Indian Tomb*, 1921), and in Murnau's *Phantom* (1922). But these women were not quite the commodities that we now think of when we employ the term 'star'. Their names were not considered sufficient to attract huge audiences and the press had barely begun to wake up to the possibility that a newly-literate generation might want to read about the lives of these women, whilst others would pore over photographs of their pin-up darlings.

Slowly the mechanisms to generate this kind of adulation fell into place, with the giant Ufa studio best placed in terms of finances and influence to achieve it. Actors such as Asta Nielsen, Lil Dagover, Gerda Maurus and Brigitte Helm all became the object of carefully-orchestrated press exposure and publicity campaigns. Yet the roles they played were, perhaps unsurprisingly given the period discussed here, of a rather unchallenging and stereotypical nature. Brigitte Helm frequently reprised elements of her standard role, as seen in Lang's *Metropolis*, playing roles which embodied the dichotomy at the heart of the female star in general: playing either the Madonna-like virgin or the whorish vamp (both as fantasy elements of the male spectator's imagination).

Virgins and vamps

One inescapable facet of the fortunes of the female stars in Weimar films and elsewhere was the restrictive nature of the roles they were to play. The studios had very clear ideas about what audiences wanted of their female leads and the directors were happy to comply. Thus Henny Porten and Pola Negri are largely passive leads in Lubitsch's historical epics, while Lil Dagover's character is merely the object of rivalry between the two men in *Dr Caligari*, panicked by the sight of Cesare's stiff body. Likewise, Ellen (Greta Schröder) is a victim of her society's repressed attitudes to her sexuality in *Nosferatu*: she must sacrifice herself in exchange for a moment of liberation, and in doing so she saves her town.

Particular attention should be paid to Brigitte Helm's dual role in *Metropolis*, which neatly sums up many of the inconsistencies evident in the portrayal of the feminine in much of Weimar film. As the pious Maria, urging the workers not to rebel, she is considered a challenge to the ruling classes who decide they must annul the threat she poses through her popularity. When she is transformed into the robot who incites the workers to revolt, she becomes at the same time the object of voyeuristic attention when she dances (like the biblical Salome), before the dandies of the city. Ultimately, her femininity poses a threat to all in the city and she brings the (male dominated) society to its knees. In a telling reflection of the role of the female star in cinema, Lang depicts the (male) audience in the nightclub growing increasingly abstracted as they lust over her provocative gyrations until they form a montage of eyes dissolved over her near-naked body. Maria (like the actor portraying her) thus becomes little more than a sexual commodity for the pleasure of the (male) gaze (as discussed in chapter 4).[3] Clearly the roles the female stars played on the screen, and indeed the roles they played in reality for the fans, gave little scope for a more serious study of the woman in Weimar society. Almost exclusively

The realm of the gaze: the robot-Maria performs before nightclub patrons

the female characters of the early films were either passive, stereotypically feminine virgins, *ingénues* at the mercy of a predatory male society or else they were rapacious vamps, posing a threat to the patriarchal order and requiring eradication.[4]

One director who chose to explore the complexities of the female psychology in rather greater detail than had hitherto been the case in Weimar film was G. W. Pabst. Pabst had been a theatrical actor and director in the early years of the twentieth century before turning to film, and he brought with him not only a fine appreciation for the advantages of the young medium over the established practices of the theatre but also a highly-developed sensibility for the injustices apparent in post-Wilheminian, Weimar society. As a representative of the expressionist era of filmmaking in Weimar, Pabst is pre-eminent as the director who utilised the medium to explore the psychology of the characters he brought to the screen. 'Pabst at his best', enthuses Paul Rotha,

> unhampered by limitations, uncut save by himself, is perhaps the one genius of the film outside Soviet Russia ... Investigation of his methods is difficult, complex, and hard to express in words. Pabst possesses a power of penetration into the deepest cell of human behaviour, and succeeds in psychologically representing the traits of his characters by filmic exposition. (1967: 263)

G. W. Pabst and the psychology of the female

Born on 27 August 1885, Georg Wilhelm Pabst initially attended a technical school in Vienna, emulating his engineer father. He disappointed his parents, however, by transferring to the *Akademie der bildenden Kunst* (Academy of Fine Arts). After graduating, he began to work as an actor in various repertory groups until joining a company which took him to the USA and the *Deutsches Volkstheater* in New York.

A trip back to Europe in 1914, initially to recruit new talent to the company, proved ill-fated since he became caught up in the outbreak of World War One. On the eve of hostilities he was arrested in France (Fritz Lang had likewise related how he had barely succeeded in escaping to Germany – see chapter 4), and was interned for the duration of the war, where he experienced a large measure of human suffering at first hand. Upon his release in 1918 he became director of a Viennese theatre but quickly moved to Berlin to embark upon a new career in film. Initially he appeared in a number of films (for example, *Im Banne der Kralle* (*Under the Spell of the Claw*, Carl Fröhlich, 1921), starring Gustav Diessl), then wrote a number of screenplays for Fröhlich before being offered the direction of *Der Schatz* (*The Treasure*) in 1923.

This was followed by *Gräfin Donelli* (*Countess Donelli*, 1924), with Henny Porten as the lead. The film was a success at the box office but it appeared to leave Pabst unsatisfied. His experiences in the USA and France had given him a strong sense of social justice and he was certain that he could make a valuable contribution to social change through the medium of film. Thus his next film, entitled *Die freudlose Gasse* (*The Joyless Street*, 1925) highlighted the social strictures condemning the characters played by Asta Nielsen and Greta Garbo to a life of misery in a society where acquisitiveness and lust are the new moral imperatives. Women are forced to offer their bodies to powerful and/or rich men, in exchange for food or money, while the men are oblivious to (or unconcerned about) the demeaning way that the women in their midst are treated. In a scene which made the studio rather nervous, Pabst signals his intent in film when Emil Jannings' predatory butcher, who demands sexual favours from women in return for his wares, is finally murdered by one of his victims.[5] Lee Attwell notes Pabst's extraordinary eye for the small details which rendered his films so expressive, stating that *The Joyless Street* was already suffused with 'the licentious atmosphere and claustrophobic décor for which Pabst was to become famous' (1977: 31). At a time when Expressionism in the arts was giving way to a more nuanced, realist approach to art in the *neue Sachlichkeit* movement (new objectivity – see chapter 6), Pabst seemed to have found a template for socially-committed filmmaking which nevertheless appealed to audiences. Although the financial backers at the studios were reticent to authorise Pabst's unconventional projects, they could not ignore his success at the box office. Now firmly established as a director with a unique eye for realism, who nevertheless imbued his films with great imagery and coded meaning, Pabst went on to film two further successes: *Die Geheimnisse einer Seele* (*Secrets of a Soul*, 1926), a psychological study of one of Sigmund Freud's cases, and *Die Liebe der Jeanne Ney* (*The Love of Jeanne Ney*, 1927) a melodrama set against the historical backdrop of the Soviet revolution.[6] The latter film focuses on the fortunes of Edith Jehanne's eponymous heroine, Jeanne, who is torn between her love for the young Bolshevik Andreas (Uno Henning) and revulsion towards the Revolution which has already claimed her father's life. Returning to her native Paris, she works for her uncle and befriends his daughter, the blind Gabrielle (played by Brigitte Helm in a finely-wrought performance). She is horrified to discover that the malicious Khalibiev (Fritz Rasp), the reporter who first betrayed her father to the Bolsheviks, is now wooing the unknowing Gabrielle. He then murders Jeanne's uncle and frames Andreas for the murder; once Jeanne discovers the villain's true actions she confronts him and effects his arrest. Apart from anything else, this film stands out because of the central role of the character of Jeanne, who is instrumental in moving the plot along, and only occasionally reverts to stereotype, such as when she stands by, powerless to prevent her father's death. It turned out that this portrayal of a stronger female character was merely an early experiment in portraying the female psyche on the screen.

In his next film, *Abwege* (*Crisis*, 1926),[7] Pabst again based the plot around the psychological issues of the central character, a young bride (Brigitte Helm once again) who quickly finds the ardour of her husband (Gustav Diessl) cooling as he works long hours to provide her with all the luxuries he believes she needs. Torn between loyalty to her husband and her own lack of sexual fulfilment she embarks on an affair. Only later does she realise that her actions have not resolved the problem, namely that in actuality what she wants is for her husband's passion to be rekindled, and returns to him to try to save their marriage. Although the plot may seem a little contrived now, and certainly could not be described as an early feminist film (since Helm returns to her husband, craving his affection), it highlights Pabst's continuing tendency to foreground the female character and explore her motivations and desires. Paul Rotha was convinced by this preoccupation of Pabst's, stating that 'his stories have been but a framework of incident on which to wind the theme of feminine character development'. Each of his female protagonists, he goes on to say,

> has had a curious, unnameable and hopelessly indefinable quality about her. He seems ... to be able to bring to the surface the vital forces of their being [and] contrives by some unknown force to invest his characters with a quality of intense feeling, with strangely complex sexual or mental significance. (1967: 269)

As Pabst's career progressed it was clear that he was developing a critical eye for the portrayal of individuals – particularly women – in crisis. Caught between the old world values of the pre-World War One Wilhelminian era and the hedonistic atmosphere of Weimar, Pabst saw women as individuals in their own right. Typically he filmed them in a far less sentimental light than his contemporaries and was less inclined to frame them as merely responsive to male-determined inputs. Pabst's women are rarely puppets or playthings, beholden to the whim of the men to whom they owe everything. In stark contrast to the Maria-automaton, discussed previously, Pabst's female leads are living, breathing, thinking personalities in their own right: not necessarily liberated, but not meekly subservient to male fantasies or indeed to a sense of fate either. Encouraged by earlier successes, he embarked on a project to film Frank Wedekind's sexually explicit and highly controversial plays *Erdgeist* (*Earth Spirit*, 1895) and *Pandora's Box* (1904)

Louise Brooks and Pandora's Box

Wedekind's plays had already generated enormous controversy in Wilhelminian Germany thanks to their combination of explicit sexuality and social critique. His notoriety had been established by the 1891 play *Frühlings Erwachen* (*Spring Awakening*, 1891), and *Earth Spirit* resulted in court cases and censorship to rival the scandal which dogged Oscar Wilde's libel case in Britain during the infamous Queensbury trials of the same year. This controversy was repeated when *Pandora's Box* once again explored the themes of unrestrained sexuality and social hypocrisy in 1904. The salacious nature of the portrayal of human sexuality in general, and female sexuality in particular, both disgusted and delighted audiences.[8]

Pabst himself had directed a stage version of *Earth Spirit* several years beforehand and had determined to make a film-version of the play. It was recognised that the role of Lulu herself was seminal to the film's success. His assistant, Marc Sorkin agreed, allegedly claiming: 'if you find the perfect actor for the rôle, you have the film' (quoted in Atwell 1977: 52). Initially, Pabst considered the young Marlene Dietrich for the title role, as she had begun to rise to prominence in this late-Weimar period, but he rejected her on the grounds that she was too overtly sexual for the character he had in mind.[9] Instead, a chance viewing of a Howard Hawks film, *A Girl in Every Port* (1928) brought the relatively unknown Louise Brooks to his attention.

Brooks had encountered a mixed reception to her films in her native America and had grown disenchanted with the Hollywood dream. As she later recalled, she was flattered by Pabst's approach to appear in his film:

> In Hollywood, I was a pretty flibbertigibbet whose charm for the executive department decreased with every increase in my fan mail. In Berlin, I stepped [on]to the station platform to meet Mr. Pabst and became an actress ... Everywhere I was treated with a kind of decency and respect unknown to me in Hollywood. (Quoted in Atwell 1977: 52–3)

Pabst seems to have been captivated by Brooks.[10] The mixture of innocence and allure, youthful vivacity and smouldering sexuality which seemed to emanate from the young American made her the quintessential 'it' girl.[11] With his star in place, Pabst proceeded with his project. According to Brooks herself, shooting at the Nero-Film studios in Berlin took seven weeks and cost approximately $75,000 (quoted in Sinclair 1971: 4). She marvelled at the German work ethic, where craftsmen could create sets which artfully reproduced depth and vitality where there was none – and all within a strictly controlled budget. And as far as she was concerned, the film's later success was almost entirely due to Pabst's energy and attention to detail: 'Pabst was a short man, broad-shouldered and thick-chested, looking heavy and wilful in repose. But in action his legs carried him on wings which matched the swiftness of his mind' (Sinclair 1971: 9). Here much of the promise he demonstrated in earlier films seems to have come to fruition and a number of his trademark techniques are apparent: cutting on movement,[12] the use of veiled or restricted views and selective use of the expressionist technique of *chiaroscuro* in order to convey a sense of menace or trauma. Yet when *Pandora's Box* premiered in Berlin on 9 February 1929 it was not a commercial or critical success – the commonest reaction being that a silent film could not do justice to the complexity of Wedekind's play. There is also a suggestion that domestic audiences were not entirely happy with Pabst's decision to give the lead role to an American (see Elsaesser 2000a).[13]

Pandora's Box depicts the life and death of a young hedonistic flapper, Lulu (Brooks), who makes her way through life in a rather superficial manner. To maintain an acceptable standard of living, she 'entertains' rich gentlemen. Her current patron, the rather creepy Dr Schön (Fritz Kortner) one day announces that he intends to end their liaison since he is to marry. In reality, however, Lulu proves too alluring and she seduces him backstage at a revue she is appearing in – just as Schön's fiancée finds them. Schön feels he has little choice but to marry Lulu but on the day of their marriage he is further humiliated by his young bride and tries to force her to kill herself. In the ensuing struggle, he shoots himself and Lulu is subsequently tried and found guilty of manslaughter. She escapes with Schön's son Alwa (Francis Lederer), who has always loved her, and embarks on a series of adventures until the couple try to make a living in fog-bound London. Here Lulu is forced into prostitution, despite police warnings that Jack the Ripper (Gustav Diessl) is at large in the city. Tragically, Lulu picks up the Ripper who murders the happy-go-lucky girl at the very moment when she might have found love.

Brooks recalled of the shoot how Pabst would have a very clear idea of the seminal moments in the plot (see Sinclair 1971). He would rush through many scenes with breathless efficiency but then spend a great deal of time on the key sequences, such as the liaison between Jack the Ripper and Lulu, and her subsequent murder. But the wedding-night scene in particular seems to have formed the focus of the whole film. It is apparent almost from the outset that the relationship between Lulu and Schön is going to be troubled. Early scenes confirm this impression: Lulu prophetically tells Schön that he will only be rid of her if he kills her, and whenever he tries to move out of her orbit her allure proves greater than his will to resist. The smile on Lulu's face after she contrives to be discovered in Schön's arms by his fiancée is one of pure triumph, acknowledging the power this carefree spirit wields over the men who follow her.

But on the night of their wedding the relationship between Lulu and Schön reaches its inevitable climax. In a sequence which initially borders on the farcical, Schön discovers Lulu partying with her old stooges Schigolch (Carl Goetz) and Quast (Krafft Raschig) in the bedroom. Incensed by their behaviour, he drives the two men out of his apartment at gunpoint. His perturbed guests depart and Schön is left alone with Lulu, or so he believes. When he enters the bedroom again he discovers his son cradling his head on Lulu's lap, having finally revealed to her the depth of his feelings. It is a classic oedipal moment, where the father and son are competing for the love of the woman who stands in the place of Alwa's mother. The *mise-en-scène* of this sequence is a striking example of expressionist *chiaroscuro* lingering into later Weimar films to achieve a particular effect, both reflecting the inner turmoil of the characters involved and creating an atmosphere of liminal spaces, where almost supernatural forces lurk in the shadows. We see Lulu, bathed in light as

The consequences of
unbridled sexuality

Alwa rests his head on her lap (in a classically Freudian pose of regression). Unexpectedly Schön looms out of the darkness, the pistol in his hand glowing in the reflected light. Gripped with jealousy, Schön ejects his son at gunpoint, thus reasserting his patriarchal authority by means of a classic phallic symbol.

Pabst carefully reveals to the viewer both the extent of the characters' emotions here and the inevitability of the outcome. Lulu, believing the crisis to be over, begins to undress in front of the mirror. The rest of the room is almost entirely dark, so that Lulu does not notice Schön approaching her. She is shocked by his image appearing in the mirror's reflection. The mirror, a favoured tool of Pabst's to reflect hypocrisy, social injustice and inner psychological struggles, frames Schön's violent solution to his problem. He offers Lulu the pistol, saying: 'Take it. Kill yourself so that you don't make me a murderer as well!' In a curious parody of an embrace, filmed entirely over Schön's back so that Lulu is all but obscured by his bulk, the deranged man leans in to press the pistol to her body. They struggle, as Lulu pleads with Schön to no avail. Then, without warning (there is no sound, of course), Schön stiffens, and wisps of smoke rise up from between the two: the bullet Schön intended for Lulu has hit him instead. Laura Mulvey once defined the essentially male-dominated position of the gaze and seeing as an active/passive relationship: 'In a world ordered by sexual imbalance, pleasure in looking has been split between active/male and passive/female. The determining male gaze projects its fantasy onto the female figure' (1989: 19). In *Pandora's Box* the mirror reflects the standard societal concept of male dominance back on itself. Schön, who could not abide Lulu's self-asserting gaze therefore resolves to kill her, but the act is turned upon himself instead. Thus, the relationship between the scopophilic (the pleasure in watching from a position of power) and the narcissistic (pleasure derived from seeing oneself, thus creating and fuelling the ego) is inverted, and Schön dies.

Brooks remembers how Pabst wanted to prevent this scene from descending into melodramatic farce. Fritz Kortner was a classical actor with very clear ideas about how such a death scene should be played. He had even deliberated over the temperature of the chocolate in his mouth which would spill out to simulate blood in his final death throes. Pabst wanted none of that and deliberately called for these scenes to be shot out of sequence, focusing on key images such as the wisps of smoke and demanding an entirely naturalistic approach to the sequence. In this way Pabst combines the expressionists' use of *chiaroscuro* with the later realist approach of New Objectivity (to be discussed in more detail in chapter 6) to create images of pure artistry, underscoring his belief that the junction between real life and the world of the psyche was where true cinematic beauty lay.

What this scene reveals is how Lulu is portrayed not as a monster in the classical sense, but as a force which negates attempts to control her in a society dominated by the phallocentric order (see Mulvey 1989). In the original classical tale of Pandora, her box unleashes its awful contents only when man (*sic*) opens the lid, just as Lulu's terrible power (as seen from a male perspective) afflicts those men who wish to possess her. Unlike Caligari or Nosferatu, Lulu rarely engineers a situation which results in the demise of her partners. Instead she is as much a victim of circumstance as all the others; the only (crucial) difference we observe is how talented Lulu is at relying upon her own talents – mainly her irresistible sexual appeal – to save her. In the courtroom scene Lulu is shocked when she is told that she has been found guilty of manslaughter, but it is Geschwitz (Alice Roberts) who creates the scene which leads to the fire alarm diversion and allows Lulu to escape. Time and again we are reminded of the concept of fortune and chance, such as when Casti Piani (Michael von Newlinsky) discovers her and Alwa on the train or the games of chance in the gambling ship in France. In each case it is the people around her who manipulate Lulu into one course of action or another, and the film's core message seems to be that those whose suspect morality cause them to condemn Lulu as a monster should themselves be condemned for steering her to destruction, even as they are drawn to her disingenuous beauty.

Where Pabst's film triumphed was in its non-judgemental portrayal of Lulu, in no small measure thanks to Brooks's captivating performance. The screen is filled with Brooks's presence. She projects an uninhibited luminosity which perfectly matches the amoral good-time girl she portrays. As an audience we are privileged to see her dazzling smile from the very outset in the guise of the meter man, standing in for the middle-class viewer, momentarily privileged to catch a glimpse of the lifestyle of the rich and the glamorous. As Elsaesser suggests, he represents the (male) spectator of the film, fantasising that he, too, can inhabit this world of sexually-confident beauties (2000a: 259–92). The meter man is quickly dismissed however, for Pabst's Lulu is not a typical screen female. In much the same way that Rotwang's creation, the robot-Maria, moves effortlessly between the social classes, and entrances them all, Pabst unleashes his amoral heroine upon an audience already conditioned to expect the fantasy-female; however, the spectator is in for a shock. Lulu, as she is portrayed by Brooks, destroys social preconceptions even as she flashes one of her knowingly-innocent smiles. As Elsaesser observes: 'In *Pandora's Box* ... the perversity of sexual tastes and diversity of gender roles is entirely "natural-ised": perhaps one of the most startling and revolutionary aspects of the film' (2000a: 266).

Pabst recasts Wedekind's 'tragedy of monsters' into a modern myth about amorality and the hypocrisy of Weimar's social values. By judi-ciously ignoring those elements of the play which are stage bound, and foregrounding aspects of the narrative which can only be transmitted by the more intimate medium of film, Pabst is able to create a 'picture of the time' (to borrow the subtitle of Lang's *Dr Mabuse*). In his film Pabst reflects both the liberation of the swinging 1920s in Berlin, and the hypocrisy of those who condemned the phenomenon, but also the unease of a society uncertain of what it has unleashed, particularly in terms of the empowered female.[14] Once the box has been opened, so the legend and the film imply, it is futile to regret the release of its contents. Thus Lulu is neither vamp nor virgin, instead she stands *outside* the Maria/robot polarity discussed previously:

> Pabst sees [Lulu] as a dangerously free and alluring innocent, with-out any notion of sin in the Christian sense, and only vaguely aware of the moral consequences of her behaviour. The tragic contradic-tion in the film emerges from the discrepancy between her natural unbridled eroticism and its consequences on the behaviour of those who fall under her spell. (1977: 61)

Thus Lulu leaves a trail of broken bodies and souls in her wake as she moves through society, not because she does not care for the individuals she meets, but because she doesn't think at all. She is pure hedonism, acting without reflection or remorse, and almost without choice. After she has escaped from her trial, she takes refuge in the flat of her erstwhile patron. Initially disturbed by preceding events, she is quickly distracted, and comforted, as she flicks through a magazine proclaiming sunny holidays, enjoying the luxuriant caress of a fur coat, and accepting the cleansing invitation of a hot bath.[15] By the time Alva finds her in the flat, she is restored to her most primitive, amoral and seductive self. But the moments of vulnerability revealed by Pabst throughout the film confound any attempts to judge Lulu in an unfavourable light. As such her demise should not be seen as a form of justice, or even retribution, so much as the inevitable consequence of her atavistic lifestyle. It is perhaps fitting that she is killed by a man whom she subconsciously recognises as a soul-mate (a trans-gendered double, perhaps, in a cinematic tradition which has relied heavily upon the *Doppelgänger* in the past), himself a victim of his destructive sexuality and wanting nothing more than to find an individual perceptive enough to accept him for what he is. In the scene where Lulu takes Jack up to her room, Pabst exposes the psychology of the two lovers in an exquisite visual arrangement, once again relying heavily on careful *mise-en-scène* and *chiaroscuro* lighting. In the filthy London garret, the two negative forces seem briefly to counteract one another's destructive potential, and yet the outcome will almost inevitably be tragic. Despite his resolution to discard his knife (another classically phallic object of male aggression in this reading), Jack is dazzled by the light which falls onto the weapon, lying on the table next to them.[16] Here, Pabst's skilful manipulation of the scene, which is a stark tableaux of close-ups of Jack's face and *chiaroscuro* shadows pierced by refracted light, leaves the serial-murderer (and the audience) in no doubt as to the fate of the beautiful innocent. In a parallel to the scene of Schön's death, the camera focuses on Lulu's face while the murderer's back obscures most of her body. Even as she closes her eyes in anticipation of a kiss (and an honest kiss for once, not one which is the result of a financial transaction), her body recoils from the knife which Jack forces into her. Thus, ultimately, the male (gun/knife/ phallus) penetrates the female (box/vagina) and the patriarchal order is restored. It is, after all, the masculine which is monstrous and to be feared, not the feminine.

What is perhaps the most remarkable aspect of Pabst's film is that we see here a film which does not rely exclusively on a male point of view to paint the portrait of sexuality presented on screen. Clearly there are occasions when this conventional viewpoint is represented: mention has

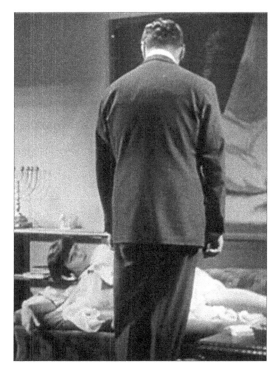

Male and female gazes: whose point of view prevails?

already been made of the meter man at the start of the film. Furthermore, when Lulu first entertains Schön in her flat the point of view is unambiguously male. Stretched out seductively on her divan in a flimsy (virginal) white flapper dress, Lulu holds her arms out to the camera, which zooms in, dragging the viewer down to the lithe, desirable body; there is no option but to succumb to her seductive charms, and her warning to Schön (which proves prophetic) applies equally to the male spectator: 'You'll have to kill me if you want to be free of me.'

Later, however, it becomes clear that the gaze that falls on Lulu can be either male or female. This radical departure is first introduced by the character of Countess Geschwitz, a friend of Lulu's who, it transpires, is in love with her. Although the early scenes with Geschwitz and Alwa still allow an ambiguous reading of the gendered gaze, it becomes increasingly clear that the spectator is invited to share the point of view of the

Countess. This becomes wholly apparent during the sequence on board the gambling ship, which is introduced to the audience wholly from the perspective of Geschwitz as she arrives on board for the first time. The camera follows her as she descends into the underworld, marvelling that Lulu has already become accustomed to its vices: 'So this is where Lulu has been these past three months', she exclaims as she enters Lulu's world. Later, Geschwitz is prepared to seduce Rodrigo Quast to save Lulu, eventually forced to kill a man just like Lulu before her. Although Geschwitz is abandoned at this stage in the film, her role in bringing a female point of view to the story is remarkable.

Pabst's amoral tale still thrills and repulses today. Perhaps part of the attraction lies in the fact that Lulu is quite so liberated. She sleeps with whomsoever she chooses and gives of herself freely and wholeheartedly, regardless of class and status. In so doing, however, she brings doom and despair to those with whom she comes into contact and eventually brings about her own death. She is the ultimate bourgeois nightmare, desireable yet refusing to conform to society's expectations so that she may better satisfy her own desires. In this way she is every bit as fascinating and repulsive in Pabst's construction as Count Orlok in *Nosferatu*. In his analysis of the film, Thomas Elsaesser notes how *Pandora's Box*, like Josef von Sternberg's later study of sexuality *The Blue Angel* stands 'in some sense paradigmatically for the period's twin identity around modernity and decadence, self-assured glamour and anxious descent into chaos' (2000a: 259).

Just a year later Pabst turned to Brooks again in *Das Tagebuch einer Verlorenen* (*Diary of a Lost Girl*, 1929), if anything an even more acerbic look at the hypocrisy lying at the centre of society's mores. When the young Thymiane (Brooks) is seduced by her father's assistant (again played by the roguish Fritz Rasp), and has a baby by him, the family choose to give the baby away and banish the young girl to a reform school. Later Thymiane escapes and becomes a successful and ultimately respectable call-girl, again unashamedly using her sexuality to establish a position for herself in society. Originally Pabst had intended for his anti-establishment heroine to end the film as a wealthy madame, unabashed at the course she has taken in society, but he bowed to studio pressure and added a happy ending where the Count marries her and her status is restored: the film remains critical of a society which chooses to deny its sexuality, to criticise those who flaunt their sexual nature and to punish those who are innocent victims of society's hypocrisy, but rather less so than if Pabst had had his way.

In later years Pabst continued to develop his sense of social responsibility. Moving even further to the political left as conditions in Weimar began to deteriorate again (precipitated by the Wall Street Crash of 1929), his subjects included a pacifist depiction of World War One (*Westfront 1918*, 1930), a study of Franco-German relations in the mining community called simply *Kameradschaft* (*Comradeship*, 1931) and a film version of Bertolt Brecht's *Dreigroschenoper* (The *Threepenny Opera/The Beggar's Opera*, 1931). Eventually though, the rise of the Nazis forced him to choose exile in Paris. He later moved to Austria and had intended to emigrate to the USA like so many of his contemporaries but the annexation of Austria by the German army prevented this. After the war he continued to make films, including a number dealing with resistance to the Nazis (most famously *Es geschah am 20. Juli* (*It happened on 20th July*, 1955)), which starred the Austrian actor-turned-director Bernhard Wicki.[17] He died in Vienna on 29 May 1967 as the result of a liver infection.

As a director engaged with the society within which he operated, G. W. Pabst was almost unique in the way he chose to use his films to hold up a mirror to the audience which came to see them. His women are deliberately portrayed rather ambiguously, at once casting off some of the stereotypical aspects of the female image in films of the day, yet still showing a male-dominated society which succeeds in asserting itself over the woman. Whether addressing issues of sexuality, as discussed here, the still-contentious issue of war and pacifism (*Westfront 1918*), or the question of class injustice in Germany (*Comradeship*), Pabst applied an artistic eye to his work which invariably led to praise from critics and box-office success, even as the studios and authorities sought to curb his social conscience. In Louise Brooks he found a young woman who embodied the carefree sexuality of Wedekind's Lulu, and created an icon which still stands today as a symbol of the chaotic period of German history between the wars. Even if *Pandora's Box* was misunderstood and dismissed in its day – Kracauer rather sniffily describes Lulu as 'a woman driven by insatiable sex lusts' and says of the director 'Pabst blundered in choosing a play that ... belonged to the fantastic postwar era rather than to the realistic stabilised period' (1947: 178–9)[18] – the film has come to enjoy a growing reputation as time has gone by. In a film which could only enhance the reputation of Weimar cinema, Pabst combines artistic integrity with social conscience, and Brooks with her androgynous bob haircut represents the hedonistic days of Weimar's golden years before social and economic conditions took a catastrophic turn for the worse.

6 STREET LIFE AND THE END OF EXPRESSIONISM: JOE MAY'S *ASPHALT* (1929)

If Weimar's first films were characterised by visions of the past, images of monsters and ghouls and coded references to the turmoil of the present, the last years of the Republic before its final and spectacular collapse were characterised by an altogether different kind of film. In response to broader artistic developments, a more socially-committed form of artistic realism and an avant-garde documentary style became increasingly popular. Although Expressionism as a cinematic force had all but disappeared by the later years of the Weimar Republic, elements of this brief phenomenon may still be discerned in films from this period. This reflects a growing sense of transition, probably present to a greater or lesser extent through-out the Weimar era, but now increasingly centring on the city as an agent of Modernism, highlighting a debate over the relative virtues and vices of the city and the country which was contentious and heartfelt. In this final phase of the Republic's tortuous existence, film found a particular niche for itself in the modernist debate.

During the second half of the 1920s Germany flourished. The tribu-lations of the early postwar years were over, and the nation as a whole seemed to be moving towards a future of stability, prosperity and progress. In social terms, the middle years of the decade had seen a significant improvement in economic conditions, partly due to the generous terms of the Dawes Plan[1] and partly thanks to the generally successful policies of Gustav Stresemann, first as Chancellor, and then as Foreign Minister. Although these conditions were not necessarily optimal for film production (since the stronger Mark made both production and overseas distribution more expensive) this resulted in a boom time in Germany, accelerating the pace of change which was apparent even in the first catastrophic years of political and economic turbulence. As the economy stabilised, so industrial capacity was optimised and conditions for the consumer improved. New roads and housing were commissioned, reinforcing the sense of recovery, and German scientists, philosophers and artists were held in high esteem on the global stage.[2] After many years of depression, suddenly it seemed as if optimism and gaiety were the order of the day.

Despite rising production costs, the middle years of Weimar saw Germany becoming established as a serious rival to Hollywood in terms of film production.[3] Thanks to a reputation for producing films which combined artistic flair and technological innovation, Germany was the dominant film nation in Europe with Ufa (as its largest studio) responsible for much of that output. But it is now clear that Ufa in particular had over-stretched itself in the struggle to maintain competitiveness. Erich Pommer, the producer who was largely responsible for Ufa's success, had been lured to Hollywood in 1926, and a large number of prominent directors, actors and technicians followed him in subsequent months and years. Pommer, at least, agreed to return to Germany in 1927, but it was clear that if Germany wanted to keep up the contest with Hollywood, it would be forced to pour vast sums of money into increasingly ambitious productions: Ufa's flagship project of 1926, Murnau's *Faust*, had failed to bring success in America, so necessary if Ufa were to avoid bankruptcy,[4] while Lang's *Metropolis* is reputed to have cost six million Marks (four times its allocated budget which was itself hugely ambitious), with no realistic chance of making a return on that sum (see Garncarz 2004). The Parufamet deal of 1925, which saw increased cooperation between Ufa, Paramount and MGM, certainly staved off disaster, bringing much-needed cash and guaranteed distribution rights in the US, but with hindsight it was clear that the terms of the deal were more beneficial to the US studios than they were to Ufa (see Kreimeier 1999: 127–8).

One response to this transatlantic battle was an attempt to emulate what was seen as the American style of filmmaking, which Paul Rotha called 'the surrender to the American cinema' (1967: 292). German film in general, and Ufa in particular, had always been attracted to the grand epic, but now its directors embraced the Hollywood narrative style of explicit causal narrative links, a preference for the shot/reverse-shot of depicting character interaction, and a predilection for the coherent, self-contained happy end.[5] Furthermore, these ideological shifts were occurring during the period when the advent of sound was just over the horizon, threatening to change the face of film at a still more fundamental level. Thus German cinematic Expressionism was coming to an end.[6] Several directors' styles were already far removed from the heady days of *Dr Caligari* or *Nosferatu*, and, once again, it was developments in the art world which seemed to be setting the tone for what proved to be the swansong of Weimar cinema.

Neue Sachlichkeit

On 14 June 1925 Gustav Hartlaub, director of the Mannheim *Kunsthalle* art gallery opened an exhibition of contemporary fine art entitled 'Neue Sachlichkeit' or 'New Objectivity'. Its subtitle, 'German Art since Expressionism' made it clear that here was a new movement, openly laying claim to be the artistic inheritor of the expressionist legacy. The warm sensuality and pseudo-religious themes of Expressionism could no longer survive in a Germany which had experienced such trauma in the war and after, they argued. In the catalogue which accompanied the first exhibition Hartlaub wrote:

What we are showing is simply the fact that art is still here, that it is struggling to establish its right to new, unspoken modes. That it still lives – despite a cultural situation which appears so antago-nistic towards the essence of art in a way which an era has rarely been before. (Cited in Fath 1994: 11)

To the advocates of this new movement the fundamental aims of Expressionism had been smashed in World War One and overwhelmed by the superficiality and consumerist drive of the Weimar period. This new generation felt that the expressionists' desire to look beneath the surface of things had been found wanting, and that now it was time to regard modern life with objectivity and dispassion. Artists whose work was presented at this early exhibition had already displayed these tendencies in the first years of the 1920s, influenced as they were by Expressionism, Dadaism and Cubism, but many of the German artists exhibited offered a more overtly political viewpoint through their work. A core of so-called 'verists', soon formed around the movement: painters such as Georg Grosz, Max Beckmann and Otto Dix, the author and playwright Alfred Döblin, and the composer Kurt Weill. The works of these artists teem with life, set as they frequently are on bustling city streets. In a strange mix of social criticism and social realism they focus on individuals such as businessmen and generals, still thriving despite the misery they are said to have inflicted on Germany, as well as beggars and prostitutes, who represent a seedier (yet more honest) side of city life. In *Metropolis* (1916), for instance, Grosz shows the bustle of a cityscape in the fractured angles of the later expressionist painters, with pedestrians reduced to abstract shapes, almost subsumed into the buildings which loom over them. In photography too, avant-garde abstraction became increasingly commonplace: Paul Citroën produced a collage of street images, entitled *Metropolis* (1923) where the images create an overwhelming montage of modernity.

At the same time these modernist tendencies began to be felt in other areas of creativity. In 1919 the hugely influential Bauhaus school was founded in Weimar by Walter Gropius and within a few years had developed into one of the key centres of Modernism in Germany.[7] The Bauhaus movement was chiefly responsible for a renewal of the suburban landscape, seeking to combine the best elements of various European arts and crafts movements with a utilitarian attitude to the need to build new, comfortable and relatively cheap housing for the masses, along with the total design concept (so beloved of many German artistic movements) which meant that interior design, furniture, even cutlery and crockery, should all be incorporated into the School's remit. In many ways, the glass and steel constructions of buildings and chairs, and the clean lines of windows and tables which emerged from the Bauhaus designers, became as much synonymous with Weimar as the paintings of Grosz and Dix or indeed the cinematic imagery of Lang or Wiene. Taken together they all speak of an embrace of Modernism, a desire to look to the future (once again) with optimism, despite the tribulations which beset Germany throughout the decade, which at least in part explains our fascination with the period.

In addition to these movements the *Großstadtroman*, or city novel, fused elements of Expressionism and other modernist traditions to embrace a nonlinear, montage style of narration which became a feature of the literature of 'New Objectivity'. This development was not unique to Germany: James Joyce's hugely influential novel *Ulysses* (1922), which was set in the city of Dublin on a single day in 1904, is generally regarded as the first example of this new style of urban storytelling, followed in the USA by the John dos Passos novel *Manhattan Transfer* in 1925. Then, in 1929, Alfred Döblin published his own take on this concept, *Berlin Alexanderplatz*, a work which stands at the very heart of the New Objectivity movement, creating a rich montage of imagery as the novel follows the fortunes of Franz Biberkopf in contemporary Berlin.

Streetlife, modernity and the metropolis

What all these elements had in common was a preoccupation with the city as the prime location of modernity and change. An ideological battle had broken out in Germany at this time, with two diametrically opposing views of society. The central point in this struggle was the binary opposition between the city and the country, a perception that the city was the centre of progress, a vibrant place of opportunity and excitement, and the counterpoint which saw the city as a direct threat to conservative values of tradition and honour, faith in God and the State, and common decency. Art was quickly marshalled into the debate, not least in the case of the cinema since, as David Clarke points out in *The Cinematic City*, 'it is unthinkable that the cinema could have developed without the city, and ... the city has been unmistakably shaped by the cinematic form' (1997: 1).

Berlin was by now regarded as one of the most vibrant locations in Europe, the centre of a nation now brimming with confidence; it appeared that the city aspired to rival the excitement generated by New York or Chicago. Of course other European capitals were flourishing as the horrors of World War One receded into the past, but many felt that Berlin alone possessed the youthful exuberance of the greatest cities across the Atlantic. Patrice Petro identifies Berlin as a nexus of chance, a place where diverse currents combine to offer virtually limitless opportunities. A contemporary essay which likens the European capitals to women makes this abundantly clear:

There is no city in the world so restless as Berlin. Everything moves. The traffic lights change restlessly ... the lighted advertisements flash. London is an old lady in black lace and diamonds. Paris is a woman in the prime of her life ... But Berlin is a girl in a pull-over, not much powder on her face. (Quoted in Petro 1989: 41)

Siegfried Kracauer, working in Berlin in the 1920s, readily acknowledged the potential offered by this metropolis. But he also cautioned against what he saw as the superficiality of a society which was characterised by glittering lights and enticing shop windows. In his 1927 essay on 'The Mass Ornament' (see 1995a) he discusses the aesthetics of modern life and how this relates to the historical processes which define a culture. He recognises the validity of the images and practices which define Weimar Germany as social objects and goes on in later essays to relate this specifically to the film. This 'calico world', as he called the film industry (referring specifically to Ufa's Neubabelsberg studios; see 1995b), was literally a chameleon, where 'everything [is] guaranteed unnatural and everything exactly like nature' (1995b: 281). The city, and its analogous counterpart, the film, appears to be all things to all observers without perhaps offering any substance to anyone. While modern Weimar society might offer great potential, Kracauer felt, it was distracted by the excess and the abstraction of society. This was nowhere more apparent than in cinema: in 'The Little Shopgirls go to the Movies' (see 1995c), also published in 1927, Kracauer demonstrates how the process of abstraction – and indeed of distraction – reached its peak: 'Films are the mirror of the prevailing society', he states, even though he acknowledges that this does not mean to say that they are necessarily realistic:

But the films do not therefore cease to reflect society. On the contrary: the more incorrectly they present the surface of things, the more correct they become and the more clearly they mirror the secret mechanism of society. In reality it may not often happen that a scullery maid marries the owner of a Rolls Royce. But doesn't every Rolls Royce owner dream that scullery maids dream of rising to his stature? Stupid and unreal film fantasies are the *daydreams of society*, in which its actual reality comes to the fore and its otherwise repressed wished take on form. (1995c: 292; emphasis in original)

Thus modern urban society, and its reflection in film, become for Kracauer akin to the bright shop windows of Berlin's main streets: exercises in wish fulfilment at a time when the country was recovering from the traumas of the War and the uneasy first years of peace. The urban melodrama is thus no more than another fantasy, a vicarious thrill for a society which now appears to specialise in thrill-seeking.

The city in film

It was not long before the fascination with the city found its way into film production. Erich Pommer identified the potential of the street for Germany's film industry: 'The street becomes the symbol of human existence – a ceaseless intermingling of destinies' (quoted in Jacobsen *et al.* 1993: 61).[8] Lotte Eisner saw a more fundamental urge behind the street films, suggesting that they continued the German preoccupation with the dark side of the soul: 'In German films the street represents the call of Destiny, especially at night' (1969: 251). When Karl Grune directed the prototype for this genre, *Die Straße* (*The Street*, 1923), subtitled 'The Story of a Night', he featured the street itself as a location for excitement, criminality, danger and even death. It was the first occasion when the street 'enters directly into the action. We first see it as a luminous temptation from a middle-class dining room' (Eisner 1969: 252). G. W. Pabst offered similar images in his film *The Joyless Street* (see chapter 5). What these films did was take the *chiaroscuro* concept of the great expressionist films and combine it with a portrayal of the urban landscape to create a place of contrasts which aptly summed up the psychological nature of the early expressionist classics. No longer did the audience have to thrill at a terror imported from abroad, such as in Murnau's *Nosferatu*, because all those extremes of emotion present in the earlier films could be generated by stories set in the dark of a city-night.

In a film such as Murnau's *The Last Laugh* a whole city-block was constructed utilising forced perspective techniques to give the shots greater depth, so that the street itself becomes an additional character. It stands as a metaphor for the whole of the Weimar Republic, a place where fortunes can be made or thrown away, reputations built up or smashed down, loves won or lost. It represents modernity and tradition clashing virtually head-on and it offers the promise of a myriad of possible futures, depending on where the observer wants to go.

In a parallel development, some directors responded to the realist intentions of New Objectivity by moving towards a documentary approach to filmmaking. Walter Ruttmann's avant-garde documentary *Berlin: Symphonie der Großstadt* (*Berlin: Symphony of a Big City*, 1927) was an innovative and highly-experimental documentary approach to the filming of the city.[9] The film presented a montage of city images with political meaning imparted by the choice of images presented, following the classic Soviet model championed above all by Sergei Eisenstein. Thus a sequence showing the purchase of a diamond necklace in a Berlin jewellery store is contrasted immediately with a beggar on the same streets. Later examples of this new approach to the city as a milieu include such influential realist films as *Menschen am Sonntag* (*People on Sunday*, 1930), and Bertolt Brecht's famous *Kuhle Wampe oder Wem gehört die Welt?* (*Whither Germany?*, 1932) featuring location shooting and non-professional actors.

In contrast to these 'absolute films' as they are sometimes called, the street film as a genre stands out primarily in its artificiality. They were all studio creations, intended to control the imagery of the narrative with as much care as the jagged sets in *The Cabinet of Dr Caligari* or the forests of Lang's *Siegfried's Death*. Ufa's Neubabelsberg studios were the site of these urban myths: 'The milieu was the street, but in the service of a symbolic exaggeration. Realism was a carefully-planned construct' (Kaes 1993: 61). The reason for this is straightforward: the street film was in actual fact still an exercise in the psyche, just like in the earliest expressionist films, an attempt to show oneiric visions, depicting the ways in which a character's surroundings could influence his or her emotions and thoughts. Even the favourite standby of expressionist film, the use of *chiaroscuro* lighting, was employed at times to demonstrate states of inner turmoil in these later films. Looking back on this era Kracauer, perhaps unsurprisingly, finds a metaphorical reading of this control which links the street films of the final days of Weimar, to the political street films of the early Nazi period:

> The imagery of the street films reveals that in the Germany of the time the street exerted an irresistible attraction. [They] figuratively express discontent with the stabilised republican regime. Life, they seem to say, is not worth while within the boundaries of the 'system'; it comes into its own only outside the rotten bourgeois world. That the centre of life is the street – a quarter peopled

not with proletarians, but with outcasts – indicates that the dis-
contented are far from being socialist-minded ... The street films
emphasise desertion of the home, but ... in the interests of authoritarian behaviour. (1947: 158–60)

The street films 'are dreamlike complexes of images constituting a sort of
secret code' (1947: 159) which reveal a grim fascination with the seedier
underbelly of the glittering world of the shop window. Audiences paid
money to view a re-creation of the street because it allowed them a glimpse
into (an imagined) soul of their city, in the same way that *Dr Caligari* had
allowed audiences to peer into the troubled soul of poor, mad Franzis. This
vicarious thrill, at a time when the Republic was enjoying relative stability, goes a long way towards explaining the appeal of the street film. As
Kracauer noted of *The Street* at the time of its release, the street film is
a 'silent, soulless coexistence of controlled vehicles and uncontrolled
desires' (quoted in Kaes 1993: 60).

Joe May and Asphalt

Asphalt came at the very end of the period of Weimar film, just as the
advent of sound, and then the rise of the Nazis, changed everything. Its
director, Joe May, had been one of the founding figures in the German film
industry, directing his first film, *Die Fahrt nach Hamburg* (*The Journey to
Hamburg*) in 1911, and over eighty films in total by the time of his death in
1954. Another Austrian by birth, like Fritz Lang and G. W. Pabst, May was
born Joseph Mandl on 7 November 1880, in Vienna. After completing his
university studies in Berlin, he began working in theatre, directing operet-
tas in Hamburg, and later married the actress Mia May (whose surname he
took) in 1902.

May first came to prominence as a director before World War One with
the successful 'Stuart Webbs' detective series in 1914. Titles such as *Die
geheimnissvolle Villa* (*The Mysterious Villa*, 1914) and *Der Spuk im Haus
des Professors* (*The Ghost in the Professor's House*, 1914) give a fair indication of the films' generic credentials and staple plots. Apart from a brief
spell in the army, May continued to direct films in the war years, initially for
his own production company 'Joe May-Film', and later for Ufa. After the war
he devised another successful detective series, based around the equally

imaginatively-named English detective Joe Deebs. He quickly established himself as a director of some talent when it came to multi-part adventure stories, often set in exotic locations. First came the epic *Veritas Vincit* (1919), starring his wife in the lead role as a woman who must endure challenges and hardships before truth does, as the Latin title suggests, triumph. Two further adventure series cemented his reputation, firstly the *Herrin der Welt* series of 1919 (eight films in total), and then the two-part *Das indische Grabmal* (*The Indian Tomb*, 1921).

May was, by all accounts, quite a showman who had bluffed his way into the business and was now busy making his way to its pinnacle. He was clearly a flamboyant character who considered himself good at sport and would think nothing of taking a two-day trip to London to buy some new shirts (see Borgelt 1993: 58–9, 69). After the heady days of success during and immediately after the war, however, May seems to have faded from view somewhat. There is some evidence that the exotic films which had made his reputation gradually fell from favour. He continued to direct films such as *Der Farmer aus Texas* (*The Farmer from Texas*, 1925) and *Heimkehr* (*Homecoming*, 1928) with mixed success. These films reveal a move towards greater realism and a tendency to experiment with new camera booms and dollies (no doubt inspired by Murnau's 'unchained camera'), which saw the introduction of a new kind of camera dolly in *Asphalt*. But he should also receive credit for his discovery of the young Fritz Lang, who was May's favoured scriptwriter in the early days, even if Lang eventually felt that May was holding him back (see chapter 4). It also seems likely that May gave Marlene Dietrich her first acting role in the 1922 film *Tragödie der Liebe* (*Tragedy of Love*), according to Klaus Kreimeier, 'a potboiler of a mystery story involving a murdered count, a boxer, and a cheerful coquette' (1999: 150).

May had one thing in common with many of his contemporaries in the Weimar film industry – he was a Jew. Anti-semitism was growing, and the takeover of Ufa by the prominent right-wing industrialist Alfred Hugenberg in 1927 might well have seen this prejudice gradually increase. May moved his filmmaking talents to Paris, and by 1933 to Hollywood but he never really settled there. Although he directed a small number of modestly successful B films in Hollywood, such as *Music in the Air* (1934) and *The Invisible Man Returns* (1940), his career rather petered out. For a decade before he died in 1954, he and his wife tried to make ends meet by running a restaurant in Hollywood called 'The Blue Danube' (see Elsaesser 2000b: 375).

If May's career was disappointing compared with his more illustrious contemporaries such as Lang or Murnau, it must be pointed out that in *Asphalt* he gave Weimar cinema a fine, late, silent movie – at the point when the advent of sound was changing all the rules – as well as a prime example of the street film, with minimal use of intertitles during numerous long sequences. It is also a fascinating attempt to combine the objectivity of the avant-garde documentary makers with Ufa's great demand for American-style melodramas, even if the attempt does not always succeed. Although we can no longer be talking here of an expressionist film, it is significant that a number of expressionist elements – not least the use of *chiaroscuro* lighting – can be observed throughout the film.

Working from a script co-written by May, shooting of *Asphalt* took place in Ufa's Neubabelsberg studios during the Autumn of 1928, using a cast of relative unknowns: the German-born American actress Betty Amann, who plays the charlatan Else, and Gustav Fröhlich who had come to prominence as the young Freder Frederson in Lang's *Metropolis* and had appeared in May's *Heimkehr*. He was gaining a reputation as a fresh-faced ingénue, which was perfect for this tale of innocence and morality.

Production stills reveal the lengths May and his designer Erich Kettelhut went to, in order to build a faithful recreation of a busy Berlin street within Ufa's great hangars (see Müller 1994: 59). This might seem surprising when one considers that the real thing was available only a few minutes away but is typical of the Weimar filmmakers' determination to retain control of virtually every aspect of filmmaking. The premiere was held on 11 March 1929 in the Ufa-Palast am Zoo in Berlin, and the film was apparently well-received (see Hake 2002: 45), probably due at least in part to May's previous reputation as a director of exotic thrillers.

On the surface at least, *Asphalt* is a straightforward melodrama of innocence and conscientiousness ruined by sexuality and base morality. Young police officer Albert Holk (Fröhlich) is a dedicated guardian of the law. He loves his assignment as a traffic policeman on Berlin's busy streets, creating order out of chaos. His duty station is an intersection where seemingly the whole world flows by. Holk is part of the machinery of this modern environment, as vital to its continued function as the oil and engines of the vehicles and the drivers behind the wheels. He is content and entirely in control of his situation.

From the start, however, there is an indication that this world of movement and light is not entirely benign (even if we choose to ignore our modern horror of the pollution which pours out of every vehicle!).[10] As pedestrians window-shop, a pair of pickpockets callously identify and isolate a woman before emptying her purse of its contents. The urban jungle is not so different from the animal world after all.

Things begin to go wrong when a request to intervene in a suspected theft from a jewellery store brings Holk face to face with the vivacious thief Else Kramer (Amann). She has already used her sensuality to guile the elderly store owner; her glittering smile as artificial and superficial as the light flashing off the diamonds she covets. Once she is unmasked, though, she sobs a story of rent arrears and threatened eviction. Torn between duty and temptation, Holk battles with his conscience, and loses. Naively he allows her to stop at her flat – supposedly to pick up her identity papers – where she seduces him and his downfall is assured.

Holk chooses to believe Else's story of desperation, although the audience is privy to moments when Else reveals her genuine love for Holk. But the inevitable crisis is triggered by the arrival of Else's lover and criminal boss. Holk fights and kills the older man. Distraught, he confesses the deed to his policeman father, who dutifully escorts his son to the station.[11] Only the timely intervention of Else, who confesses everything, prevents Holk from going to jail. As she is led to the cells, the young man declares that he will wait for her until her release.

From the opening credits May sets the tone for the central concept in the film: the street is viewed as the nexus of all possible futures, with opportunities radiating away from the intersection in all directions. The documentary-style opening montage of workers pouring steaming asphalt onto the ground, then pounding it with their tools, seems to prefigure the labouring chaingangs of the deep South in a low-budget Hollywood *noir* thriller, while the rhythmic pounding and the hiss of steam suggest to us perhaps that it is the lure of sex – in the guise of the archetypal vamp – which will cause the downfall of the upright young police officer, even as the letters of the film's title are emblazoned across the screen. The audience is left in no doubt that the tarmac poured over the earth, the most literal component in the urbanisation process, is the stage upon which this urban melodrama is played out. Thus the layers of asphalt which cover a city street act as a metaphor for the complex psychological layers of the characters in the film, as well as the layers of attraction which form the central concept.

Else Kramer:
temptation on
the streets

Almost as soon as the title has been revealed, this sequence blends into a montage of city images. A large city square is depicted, replete with advertising hoardings, where trams, buses and cars, ceaselessly criss-cross the space. The impression is of nervous, breathless energy, rein-forced by a dissolve which introduces a kaleidoscope of images moving from the corners to the centre of the screen whereupon the camera takes off on a long, looping, tilting race through the city.

Only when this sensory overload gives way to a study of the central character in the film, the young police officer, standing in the centre of the road junction, does the audience begin to comprehend how all this cease-less energy can act upon an individual. It is at this junction that Holk first encounters the 'classy demimondaine' (Kreimeier 1999: 171) Else Kramer, the irresistible nemesis who triggers his demise. He, like the jewellery store owner a few moments before, is powerless to resist her feminine wiles. Even as they enter her flat it is quite apparent that his resolve will crumble in the face of such innocent guile and unbridled sexuality. With her face initially framed by the rim of her pure white cloche, Else seems to be a sister to Lulu in Pabst's *Pandora's Box* (see chapter 5), whose smile can melt the sternest heart but whose sexuality poses a serious threat to the men who fall for her charms. The authoritarian image of Holk pacing up and down in Else's flat in his smart uniform and leather boots is immediately undermined by the fact that he is holding her little umbrella (evidence in her arrest). Then, Else appears in her negligee (black, in contrast to her all-white street attire) and her slim legs wrap provocatively around Holk's legs as she begs him not to take her to the police station; the policeman is powerless to resist. The camera pans away from the embracing couple, lingering on Holk's helmet, which has rolled across the carpet, a symbol of his capitulation and emasculation at the moment of sexual ecstasy.

Central to the image of the street in *Asphalt* is the cinema. In many of the street scenes the 'Universum' theatre lies in the background of the shot, bright and inviting. It stands directly opposite the jewellers where Holk meets Else, and forms a rather eloquent comment about the nature of film itself in the Weimar era. Here we see a knowing reference to the very location where the audience is watching *Asphalt*, an example of self-reflexivity which is common these days, but all the more remarkable for the acknowledgement that at the heart of the city portrayed on the screen is the cinema to which the audience has gone to experience the street.[12]

There are layers of attraction at work in *Asphalt* which go to the very heart of the cinema of attractions itself. The images on the screen centre on the gaze, on longing and on the desire to possess. The characters are like magpies, drawn to those things which gleam and entice. Note how the entire film is shot through a gauzy filter which allows light to sparkle provocatively.[13] The street itself is the location for many or all of these layers of attraction: initially Else Kramer (whose name has connotations with the German words for 'magpie' and 'hoarder') is attracted to the glittering diamond; Albert Holk is in turn attracted to the glamorous young thief (indeed he is prepared to risk his liberty to have her); the pedestrians who populate Holk's world are drawn to the bright lights of the shop windows which line the (artificial) streets of Berlin on the screen. Beyond the imagery of attraction within the narrative there is also that of the rural peasant who is attracted to the bright lights of the city itself; and ultimately there is the film's audience, in the final layer, who succumb to the cinema's posters and bright lights and buy a ticket to sit in the dark, attracted by the images of beautiful people flickering on the screen. Crucially, each and every one of those layers seems to contain an inherent, implicit thrill associated with the fact there is equally an inherent danger in the attraction.[14] Just as *Dr Caligari* was a cinematic experiment to externalise psychological fears, in

The Universum cinema in *Asphalt*: the source of attraction

a plot which flirts with attraction and repulsion, sanity and madness, so *Asphalt* uses the external location of the street to show Holk's descent into the depths – linking directly to the Romantics of the nineteenth century whose notions inspire so much of Weimar cinema. Thus the brief echoes of Expressionism's *chiaroscuro* effects, which are so clearly present, for example, in the stairwell when Holk senior accompanies his son to the police station, reveal that thematically *Asphalt* is as much an expressionist film as *Dr Caligari*, even if the visual mode of representation has changed in the intervening years.[15] Even though this film is a prime example of a street film, coming as it does at the very end of the era known as Weimar film, May's preoccupation with his characters' inner world is as compelling as was Wiene's. The allegorical qualities of these films still comes to the fore, despite the realist approach of May or Pabst, and even the apparently incongruous happy end (in this case the fact that the diamond thief has a heart of gold, and is prepared to go to jail to preserve the reputation of her young lover) fits in with a pattern of studio-directed wish-fulfilment which rarely fully satisfies today.

Petro identifies the representative nature of these street films thus: 'Characters in the ... street film are often so typological that their exaggerated gestures and expressions must be read for how they charge the narrative with an intensified significance, with meaning in excess of what the narrative depicts' (1989: 31). Like the countess in Lang's *Dr Mabuse*, who is attracted to the thrills of the gambling den, the audience is seduced by the bright lights of the street in the same way that the naïve Holk succumbs to the charms of the girl. The warning of the street film is that the fantasy can go easily wrong – the street is, after all, the haunt of murderers, magpie thieves, confidence tricksters and seductresses. But then again, surely that is part of the attraction?[16] Even as the period of Weimar cinema, and the expressionist film, drew to a close, the filmmakers' preoccupation with the psychological make-up of their characters continued virtually unabated. Together they explored the oneiric world of dreams and visions, and the liminal spaces on the fringe of society, where light and darkness meet. On the threshold of the talkies, and of the rise of the Nazis, May and his contemporaries revelled in the imagery of German city life, creating some of the finest images produced at any time in the Weimar cinema and gave to world cinema a rich legacy of classic images which abide today.

CONCLUSION: WEIMAR CINEMA'S FLIGHTS OF FANTASY

Films are, almost by their very nature, the product of an entertainment industry, and as such those which emerged from Germany during the years of the Weimar Republic are no exception. It would be a mistake, however, to conclude from this assertion that they have little or no value to students of film today. Instead, the films represent in their entirety a marvellous image of a remarkable society undergoing rapid social, economic and political change. As a document of their time, as well as prime examples of the development of film into an established art form in its early years, Weimar's expressionist films exert a constant and entirely justified fascination even today.

The films selected for study in this volume have presented the reader with a broad impression of the extraordinary creativity of this remarkable era. Yet one of the difficulties encountered when studying Weimar film is precisely its diversity. Countless observers, not least Siegfried Kracauer, attempted to divine a kind of meta-text of Weimar cinema, to create homogeneity out of the chaos by selecting films and scenes which fit neatly into a given approach to the subject, whilst underplaying (or even ignoring) others which threaten to undermine a given thesis. Such critics trace the development of expressionist film as a continuous process, whereby certain signature elements are foregrounded as evidence of Weimar cinema's coherence: the avant-garde *mise-en-scène*, the socio-political content or the director's *auteurist* influence, to name just three. In the main, studies of Weimar film have chosen to overlook the puzzling contradictions and inconsistencies apparent within the industry, and even within some films. Thus the subject has exerted a strange fascination on scholars, students and cineastes alike, whilst continuing to frustrate them in almost equal measure.

After the important work undertaken by Siegfried Kracauer and Lotte Eisner in particular, to establish the academic study of Weimar cinema, Thomas Elsaesser, in his seminal *Weimar's Historical Imaginary*, greatly developed our understanding of the expressionist films of the era when he chose to tackle the various flaws and inconsistencies head-on. Summing up the cinema of the Weimar Republic as 'impersoNation' [*sic*] (2000a: 437), whereby the cinema borrows eclectically from all areas of society in an attempt both to reflect, and to mould, the prevailing cultural patterns, he describes this process as 'a kind of dance on the volcano [which] makes available the iconography of the nation or the fantasises of the national history as counterfeit signs for a festival, a carnival' (ibid.). Only relatively recently have Elsaesser and others come to realise that Weimar film, in all its glorious inconsistency, must be seen as part of a longer tradition of filmmaking in Germany. Valuable work is now being carried out on the German cinema of the pre-World War One era, as well as that of the Nazi era (avoiding the temptation to dismiss the latter as no more than odious propaganda), providing an important contextual and cultural reference to the place of Weimar's expressionist cinema within Germany's cinematic search for identity and focus.

In a volume such as this, which stands as an introduction to this fascinating movement located within the ongoing history of German and world cinema, I have resisted the temptation to provide (or even to imply) an overarching interpretation of the films released in the period studied. Instead, each chapter has quite deliberately focused on a single aspect of a given film, genre or motif. Only now, as the study draws to a close, might I offer some broad observations, acutely aware of the many elisions and downright omissions which are a necessary part of the project's remit.

What is significant here is the extent to which filmed Expressionism is present in each of the films selected for this study. I have chosen to focus on the way in which these directors and their films present the audience with worlds where reality and fantasy coexist, where the interplay of light and shadow suggests a liminal, subjective state on the threshold of the objective world. Each film adopts the principles of Expressionism to a greater or lesser extent, but all focus on certain key features, such as the use of *chiaroscuro* lighting techniques to portray the liminality of the spaces on screen or the preoccupation with the characters' psychological condition. All rely significantly (though not always exclusively) on studio space to shoot their films since this allows them total control over all aspects of *mise-en-scène*, and all have a significant relationship with the turbulent events of the Weimar years (whether reflecting them, commenting upon them, or both).

Thus in Wiene's *Dr Caligari*, the crazy arabesques and harsh zigzags of the painted backdrops suggested a fantasy world, where the narrative is constantly undermined by suggestions that one or more of the principal characters might in fact be mad. Likewise, in Murnau's *Nosferatu* the overpowering arches and shadows of the vampire's castle suggest a *chiaroscuro* painting, laden with foreboding and doom. Moreover, the supernatural relationship between Count Orlok and Ellen, which is consummated on the night in which she sacrifices herself for the good of her home town, seems to lay the ground for Pabst's treatment of the female psyche a few years later in *Pandora's Box* (1928). Although Pabst has all but abandoned Expressionism by this time, his careful use of *chiaroscuro* elements in key sequences such as the death of Lulu's lover Schön continues the tradition perfected by Lang, where studio-bound filming allows for absolute mastery of lighting conditions to enhance the mood of fantasy and subjectivity. Thus Siegfried's ride through the primeval forests of mythology in *Die Nibelungen* sees shafts of light penetrate the murky depths of the forest floor, contrasting starkly with the forceful, civilising geometry of the Burgundian court. Similarly, the stygian gloom of the catacombs in *Metropolis* (1927) contrasts with the artificial splendour of the city above. Even when a filmmaker like Pabst signals a general shift towards realism in film towards the end of the Weimar Republic, Joe May's *Asphalt* still relies on studio lighting to illuminate his dream-like street film, revealing the fluctuating fortunes of the naïve young policeman in the great city of Berlin. When he descends the artfully-designed staircase of his apartment building, on his way to hand himself over to the police, the presence of Expressionism as a *noir* element is all too apparent. Each film, then, still acts as an oneiric vision, revealing the hopes and fears of a Republic which, with hindsight, was probably doomed from the very outset, but which nevertheless contained an abundance of verve and excitement which thrills us even today.

The Austrian writer and dramatist, Hugo von Hofmannsthal once observed that cinema has the power to act as a substitute for dreams (see 2004: 53); this statement proves particularly telling in the films of the Weimar Republic. Perhaps the fascination with the films of the expressionist movement lie in the complex interrelation between reality and fantasy evident in virtually every example. Whilst outwardly realistic, depicting a recognisable world on the screen, the expressionist film is, in actual fact, a product of a dream world, a representation of a subterranean world of hopes, fears and fantasies. Indeed, the films themselves are the product of a unique vision, a collaborative effort by teams of expert men and women who shared their enthusiasm for the new art form with their audiences. Yet this 'rebus world' as Elsaesser dubs it (2000a: 158) rather playfully turns out to depict reality most acutely, laying bare the fundamental concerns and aspirations of the Weimar Republic, charting its difficult birth, its gradual stabilisation and its sudden and catastrophic collapse in a way that no other national film industry has achieved. In expressionist cinema, according to Susanne Langer, 'the camera is in the place of the dreamer' (quoted in Prawer 1980: 186). Thus, the threshold worlds which Wiene, Lang, Murnau and their fellow directors created can be seen even today as places where the boundary between light and darkness appears fluid, arbitrary and designed to conceal almost as much as it reveals. Ultimately in Weimar films, these worlds of light and shadow, of fantasy and reality, show us a place where dreams and truth converge in some of the most abiding images produced in the history of film to date. Slowly we are drawing closer to the centenary of the release of Robert Wiene's *The Cabinet of Dr Caligari* (1920), which heralded the advent of German expressionist film; as previously lost films are rediscovered and incomplete films are restored, our fascination with the images of Weimar's expressionist cinema can only grow more intense in the years to come.

NOTES

introduction

1 In recent years a growing debate has emerged about the relevance and validity of these two terms; see, for example, Elsaesser (2000a: 18 ff). These terms themselves reflect the growing conviction that the prodigious output of Weimar Germany's film industry defies easy categorisation.

2 Indeed, so resonant have such images become in the early twenty-first century that, significantly, the climactic scene of *Spider-Man* (2002) had to be hastily reshot in the aftermath of 9/11, since it took place on and around the towers themselves. The fact that a number of films then went on explicitly to examine the 9/11 attacks only goes to prove the point that any event of global consequence is likely to reappear in the cinema in due course. Thus, even the absence of explicit onscreen imagery invites the assumption that such a massive event can have a pervasive influence on the cinema of its day, both in terms of production as well as audience reception.

3 See particularly 'The Little Shopgirls go to the Movies' in Levin 1995: 291–304.

4 Barry Salt (1979) identifies precisely six truly expressionist films: *The Cabinet of Dr Caligari*, *Genuine* (1920) and *Raskolnikov* (1923), all directed by Robert Wiene; *Von Morgens bis Mitternachts* (*From Morn to Midnight*, Karl Heinz Martin, 1920); *Torgus* (Hanz Kobe, 1921); and *Das Wachsfigurenkabinett* (*The Waxworks*, Paul Leni, 1924). Salt also allows Fritz Lang's *Metropolis* as a possible additional candidate. All

others he considers, at best, 'expressivist'. Some critics, on the other hand, can include as many as forty or fifty titles in their lists. This is, of course, in no small measure due to the uncertainty over the definition of Expressionism itself.

5   Perhaps this explains too our fascination with a character like the vampire Count Orlok in *Nosferatu*, who repels even as we are drawn to him, and who is both blessed and cursed with immortality.

6   Berge was referring specifically to Fritz Lang's *Die Nibelungen* (1924). Lang's film was a two-parter (released in February and April). The first was released as both *Die Nibelungen: Siegfried* and *Die Nibelungen: Siegfrieds Tod* (*Siegfried's Death*); the second was released as *Kriemhilds Rache* (*Kriemhild's Revenge*). Except where both parts are examined separately (see chapter 4), general discussions of the films will use the main title, *Die Nibelungen*.

7   I am in good company here, since Thomas Elsaesser also uses these dates in his study (2000a), whilst admitting that 'the periodisation of German cinema is one of the most vexed questions in film history' (2000a: 57, note 74).

chapter one

1   Skladanowsky's 'Bioscop' was a rather cumbersome affair in comparison to the Lumières' apparatus, which explains why the German's contribution to film history has faded somewhat; see Bordwell & Thompson 1994: 8–9.

2   For recent research on this relatively neglected field, see Kessler & Warth (2002).

3   Produced as part of her doctoral research in 1913, Altenloh's *Zur Soziologie des Kinos* reported the results of questionnaires distributed to some 3000+ residents in Mannheim. Incorporating details of annual film production by nation, favourite film titles and class and gender backgrounds of the typical audience, she produced one of the first portraits of filmgoing habits. It was a groundbreaking study, published many years before any comparable study of audience demographics and viewer habits.

4   This institution formed the foundations for Weimar Germany's greatest film studio, Ufa.

5   The terms of the Allied-imposed Versailles Treaty, signed on 28 June
    1919, were deliberately intended to reduce Germany to a mere shadow
    of her former glory, stripping her of a great deal of her territories, extract-
    ing massive reparations and restricting the country's armed forces to
    almost representative levels. More controversial still was Article 231
    of the Treaty, forcing Germany to accept full responsibility for all the
    damage caused by the war. This clause, more than any other aspect
    of the Treaty, gave rise to right-wing resentment summed up by the
    so-called 'stab in the back' legend, which popularised the belief that
    politicians had sold out the undefeated German army in 1918. It was
    a major factor in the early years of unrest in the Weimar Republic, and
    was successfully exploited by Hitler in his subsequent rise to power;
    see Fulbrook 1992: 162–4.
6   I will examine this artistic phenomenon more closely in chapter 6.
7   First published in German in 1992.
8   Lubitsch's *Madame Dubarry*, released with the English title *Passion*,
    was the first German film to break into the previously closed US market,
    premiering in New York in 1920 (see Kracauer 1947: 3); for an in-depth
    examination of the impact of *The Cabinet of Dr Caligari* when it was
    screened in the USA in 1921, see Budd (1990).

chapter two

1   Although Gilles Deleuze does suggest, however, that the German
    expressionist filmmakers possessed a particularly strong sense of
    'colourism' in their creations: 'despite Griffith's and Eisenstein's
    attempts in monochrome and even in polychrome, it is undoubtedly
    Expressionism which was the precursor of real colourism in the cinema'
    (1986: 52). Of course, tinting was already well-established by the time
    Wiene's film (itself tinted on release) came out, and cine-literate audi-
    ences would have had little trouble understanding the moods evoked
    by certain standard colour tints: red for love, or danger, for example.
2   Founded by one of the pioneers of the German film industry, Oskar
    Messter, who invented the Maltese Cross for more effective advance-
    ment of film through a projector.
3   The other film being Eisenstein's *Battleship Potemkin*.
4   Adapted from the play of the same name by Paul Lindau, *Der Andere*

had already been filmed in the silent era by director Max Mack in 1913.

5   I am referring here to Fritz Lang, F. W. Murnau, G. W. Pabst and Robert Wiene.

6   This section has been adapted from my article, 'Caligari revisited: circles, cycles and counter-revolution in Robert Wiene's *Das Cabinet des Dr. Caligari*', *German Life and Letters*, 57, 2, 175–87, with thanks to Oxford University Press.

7   For a very accessible overview of the Weimar Republic see Fulbrook (2002). For an account of how films of the period responded to events on the streets, see Sandford (1995).

8   Indeed, within a few weeks of the film's première, the ultra-nationalist, right-wing Kapp Putsch in Berlin had forced the government to flee to Stuttgart and the fate of the fledgling democracy hung in the balance as mainstream army units refused to intervene against former colleagues in the 'Freikorps' militias.

9   The publication in 1995 of an original film script (belonging to Werner Krauss) revealed that Janowitz and Mayer scripted an opening scene showing the lovers happily married, some twenty years after the horrors of Caligari's Cabinet. Clearly, then, they were not interested in an ambiguous ending. Of course, Wiene retained the concept of the flashback but one which is then framed by the walls of the asylum, wherein both Franzis and Jane are apparently still confined; see Prawer (1995: 51–2).

10 The image of the organ-grinder cranking the handle of his instrument recalls the camerman operating the camera, this being just one of a number of self-referential moments in the film.

11 The *Totentanz*, or dance of death, was part religious teaching, part entertainment in medieval Germany, frequently performed at fairs and markets.

12 This motif is of course most famously taken up by Alfred Hitchcock in *Vertigo* (1958). Significantly, Hitchcock had observed, or participated in, the shooting of several German films during a visit to Berlin in 1925, when Murnau is famously supposed to have proffered the advice: 'All that matters is what you see on the screen' (see Kreimeier 1999: 102).

13 In Kafka's *Der Prozess* (*The Trial*, 1925), Josef K. is accused by faceless authority of a unspecified crime of which he is unaware. The later novel

Das Schloß (*The Castle*, 1926) shows the protagonist K. struggling to make his way through the castle of the title to deal with an insurmountable burden of administration. Both novels were written by Kafka in the early 1920s and published posthumously. Whilst it would help little to speculate whether Kafka knew of *Dr Caligari*, there appear to be some common elements in scenes, such as that of Caligari confronting the town clerk, for instance.

14 For a number of detailed accounts of the various aspects of *Dr Caligari*'s commercial success, see Budd (1990: 121–69).

chapter three

1   Among the victims of the deadly virus was the Austrian Secessionist artist Egon Schiele, who died of Spanish flu on 31 October 1918. Most commentators agree that the epidemics together killed more of the planet's population than had been killed in World War One.

2   For further reading see, for example, Kessler & Warth (2002).

3   This remake was directed by Henrik Galeen. Galeen's writing credits include *Der Golem* (*The Golem*, writer and director, 1915), *Nosferatu* and *The Waxworks*. He also directed *Alraune* (*Mandrake*, 1928), an experimental film which contains extravagant expressionistic dream sequences.

4   We should not discount the influence of horror movies which were appearing elsewhere in Europe and the US at this time, such as Carl Theodor Dreyer's *Blade af Satans bog* (*Leaves from Satan's Book*, 1921); see Prawer 1980: 8–9.

5   Note how often these themes reoccur in later films: the monster which abducts the beautiful girl features repeatedly, in *Dr Caligari* of course, but also in *Metropolis* and most famously in *King Kong* (Merian Cooper, 1933). The motif of innocence facing terror becomes the core of *Frankenstein* (James Whale, 1931) and countless imitations. Siegfried Prawer, in his study *Caligari's Children*, runs through the key motifs of horror – drawn from the earliest examples – in his chapter 'The Making of a Genre' (1980: 8–47).

6   This award was bestowed at the very first ceremony held in the Roosevelt Hotel, Hollywood on 16 May 1929. It was given the unusual title because Academy members could not decide whether to give the

Best Picture award to a commercially successful film, *Wings* (William A. Wellmann), or to recognise the artistry of *Sunrise*. For one time only they compromised and recognised both films as 'best pictures' in their own right. Janet Gaynor, who played the City Woman in *Sunrise*, was awarded Best Actress as a result of her work on several films in the preceding period.

7   For a fuller account of Murnau's life and career, see Roberts (2007).

8   These efforts proved unsuccessful. Following the release of the film Stoker's widow won a court case preventing the further distribution and screening of *Nosferatu*. All existing copies were ordered seized and destroyed and for many years the film, at least in its original form, was considered lost. Eisner investigates a re-released version of 1930, which has some synchronised sound, under the title *Die zwölfte Stunde: Eine Nacht des Grauens* (*The Twelfth Hour: A Night of Horror*). It is worth speculating that the protracted legal action may well have led to the financial ruin of Prana Film even before the case was found in favour of Mrs Stoker, thus explaining why Prana failed to produce any further films. For further reading on the subject of the film's alternative versions, and eventual restoration, see 'The Riddle of Nosferatu' in Eisner 1973: 108–19.

9   Orlok was played by the wonderfully monikered Max Schreck, whose surname means 'fright' in German.

10 Compare with the characters in *The Cabinet of Dr Caligari*, for instance, but note also the photograph of Heinrich George in Eisner 1973: 117 for a theatrical precedent.

11 Such imagery was, of course, exploited to terrible effect by the Nazis just a decade later in *Der ewige Jude* (*The Eternal Jew*, Fritz Hippler, 1940).

chapter four

1   Like the Lumière brothers, the German film pioneer Max Skladanowsky relied heavily on documentary films from the very outset of his career (see Jacobsen *et al.* 1993: 13–16).

2   These *Aufklärungsfilme* were essentially sex films hurriedly shot and released during a brief relaxation of the censorship laws.

3   Indeed, science fiction has never been a major component of German

film production: apart from Fritz Lang's *Metropolis* and *Die Frau im Mond* (*The Woman in the Moon*, 1929) notable exceptions have included *F.P.1 antwortet nicht* (*F.P.1 is Not Answering*, Karl Hartle, 1933), as well as the cult television series *Raumpatrouille Orion* (*Space Patrol Orion*), which first screened in 1966.

4   Decla-Bioscop was the studio subsequently responsible for Wiene's *Dr Caligari*. It merged with its larger rival Ufa in 1921; see Kreimeier 1999: 72–3.

5   'Karl May (1842–1912) was one of the most prolific writers of adventure stories for young people in the Wilhelminian period. His most successful were wild west tales, featuring the fictional characters of Winnetou and Old Shatterhand, which became the subject of several German films.

6   Lang appears to take the credit for inventing the concept of the countdown before blast-off, represented as it is here in visual form.

7   This is, of course, one of the very first cinematic representations of the *Dolchstoßlegende* ('stab in the back' legend), which was quickly popularised by the right-wing in postwar Germany to explain the army's failure to win the war. It is one aspect of the film's well-documented popularity with Hitler and his followers.

8   Citing the *Film Yearbook*, Kreimeier gives a figure of 244 films produced in Germany in 1925, 47 of which were Ufa productions (1999: 101).

9   These accusations were based on the similarities between Lang's soldiers forming geometric patterns and the later images of Leni Riefenstahl's *Triumph des Willens* (*Triumph of the Will*, 1934), which surely draw on Lang rather than the other way round. The fact that *Die Nibelungen* was acknowledged as Hitler's favourite film, even after Lang's decision to flee from Germany, cannot have helped the reputation of the epic in the years after 1945.

10 Think of Madonna's appropriation of the robot-Maria image in her video for 'Express Yourself' in 1989, or the design of the dystopian city in *Blade Runner*; then recall how Queen mimicked the scenes of the workers in their video for 'Radio Ga-Ga' in 1984. More recently there was the Japanese animé version of *Metropolis* by Osamu Tezuka (2001) which envisages a vertically-divided city of humans and robots, centred on a monolithic ziggurat structure which symbolises both power and hubris.

11 By the time *Metropolis* was ready for US distribution Ufa had entered into the notorious Parufamet deal; see Kreimeier 1999: 126ff.

12 It seems to me that the closest the film comes to science fiction is actually the sequence where robot-Maria makes her debut in the Yoshiwara club. She emerges from a clamshell-receptacle, its lid opening hydraulically amidst smoke and stark lighting, looking for all the world like a scene from a *Close Encounters of the Third Kind* (1980) spoof. Every time I watch the scene I almost expect the intertitle card that follows to read 'Take me to your Leader'. Lotte Eisner reveals that Lang had hoped to shoot an ending for *Metropolis* where Freder and Maria travel to another planet in a space rocket as a kind of prelude to *The Woman in the Moon* (1976: 90), so perhaps the notion of the robot-Maria's spaceship is not so far-fetched after all.

chapter five

1 The two quickly became one and the same thing as vertical production methods, pioneered by Hollywood, were introduced into German film-making and distribution.

2 Mia May married Joe May, who took her stage name upon their marriage; see chapter 6 for more details on May.

3 For an introduction to the concept of scopophilia and the male gaze in feminist cinema studies see Mulvey (1989).

4 This is not to mention the exploitation of women in the *Aufklärungsfilm*, a type of film which flourished briefly in the first two years of the Weimar Republic purporting to offer an educational content, but were invariably an excuse for nudity and other titillation.

5 This aspect of the film was so contentious that all scenes featuring the butcher were cut by several countries when it was released internationally.

6 The film was based on an Ilya Ehrenburg novel, and the studio was reportedly rather nervous of how Pabst might handle a tale of revolution but was determined to capitalise on the success of Eisenstein's *Battleship Potemkin*, which had been released in Germany the previous year to great acclaim. This is another apposite case of the film business placing commercial interests above all other considerations.

7 Also released under the title *Begierde* (*Desire*).

8 Leopold Jessner had already made a film version of the play in 1923,

released as *Erdgeist* (*Earth Spirit*). Contemporary reviews suggest that the film had lost much of the play's impact, with Asta Nielsen in the lead unable to convey the latent sexuality of Lulu.

9 Pabst was proven right, of course, for Dietrich's sexuality was what shot her to international fame just a few years later in Josef von Sternberg's *Der blaue Engel* (*The Blue Angel*, 1929) alongside Emil Jannings.

10 Pabst was not the only one: Lotte Eisner in her analysis of *Pandora's Box* enthuses about 'the miracle of Louise Brooks [who] could move across the screen causing the work of art to be born by her mere presence' (1969: 296).

11 The term was originally applied to Brooks's friend and fellow-actress Clara Bow, who had appeared in the Paramount picture *It* (Clarence Badger, 1927). The term was understood in the sense of 'she has got *it*', i.e. sex appeal.

12 A technique whereby the camera pans across a scene, following a character, and then continues to pan in the same direction in the shot which immediately follows.

13 As noted above, Pabst had considered Marlene Dietrich for the role. The anti-foreigner thesis seems unlikely, however, since Weimar cinema was already well-populated with overseas actors.

14 It is worth pointing out here that universal suffrage had been introduced in the aftermath of the collapse of the German monarchy, and female Members of Parliament were present from the outset of the Republic. As might perhaps be expected, this factor alone had caused a great deal of insecurity amongst the establishment.

15 Brooks reads a copy of *Die Dame*, one of the widest-read journals in Weimar Germany. For an examination of the role of the illustrated periodical in Weimar, and the affinities between this medium and cinema as consumer products, see Petro 1989: 110–39.

16 Pabst has dealt with a knife fixation once before, in the Freudian *Secrets of a Soul*, where repressed fears and hatred compel the protagonist to attack his wife with a knife.

17 Wicki directed *Die Brücke* (*The Bridge*, 1959) – one of the best-known German anti-war films, at least until Wolfgang Petersen's *Das Boot* (*The Boat*, 1981) – and the German sequences of *The Longest Day* (Annakin, Marton, Wicki, Zanuck, 1962).

18 Might Kracauer's objections also stem from the fact that *Pandora's Box*

is a film which sees the authority figure – Schön – overthrown by the forces of anarchy and chaos – Lulu – and thus does not fit neatly into his predeterminist theories.

chapter six

1   The Dawes Plan of 1924 was a US package of loans and renegotiated payments intended to bolster the flagging German economy, by giving her a fair chance to repay her war reparations. The later Young Plan (1929) went so far as to reduce the total payments due to the Allies, but came too late to save Germany from the worst effects of the Wall Street Crash.

2   In the period 1918–30 some fifteen German Nobel laureates were created, including Albert Einstein (1921, physics), Gustav Hertz (1925, physics) and Thomas Mann (1929, literature). Gustav Stresemann was awarded the Nobel Prize for peace in 1926.

3   Statistics provided by Hans Borgelt show that Germany typically produced more feature-length films than the USA in the years 1923–29, peaking at 242 in 1927. This is only half the story, however, since figures for screenings show that US films consistently formed the greater part of German cinemas' programmes, at least from 1926 onwards (1993: 121).

4   By the time of the premiere of *Faust* on 14 October 1926, Murnau had joined the growing ranks of directors and other filmmakers who emigrated to the USA, and never returned to Germany; see Kreimeier 1999: 118–19.

5   The twist at the end of Murnau's *The Last Laugh* has often been regarded as the epitome of the ironic take on the American happy end.

6   It should be noted here that the inheritor of filmic Expressionism in the 1930s and beyond was not in fact Germany, but America, where the *film noir* genre would be unimaginable without the many German directors, technicians and artists who formed the backbone of Hollywood's infrastructure well into the 1950s.

7   The correct name for the school was, strictly speaking, the *Staatliche Bauhaus*.

8   Having been lured to Hollywood in 1926 Pommer agreed to return to Berlin to revitalise German film prospects in the USA.

9 Ruttmann was strongly influenced by the Soviet documentary film-maker Dziga Vertov's *Kino Pravda* ('cinema of truth') movement, which resulted in the latter's celebrated *Chelovek s kino-apparatom* (*Man with a Movie Camera*) in 1929.

10 In fact the traffic fumes recall the miasmic vapours which penetrate the civilised world of the Burgundian court in Lang's *Siegfried's Death*, suggesting that Berlin is equally constructed on a framework of superficiality which is easily penetrated by baser instincts; see chapter 4.

11 The concept of authority in *Asphalt* is frequently reinforced in scenes such as the one involving Holk senior and his son, where an individual places their outstretched hand on the shoulder of another, who is literally compelled to accompany them.

12 According to a passage quoted by Kreimeier, and first published in a contemporary edition of *Film-Kurier*, there is a poster for *Asphalt* itself visible in the film: 'The play of technical possibilities, of *trompe l'oeil* and film-within-a-film techniques, is an intoxicating game for the viewer, who can yield to the momentum of the images' (1999: 171).

13 In *Asphalt* buttons, the reflections of headlights, even Else's teeth, all glitter in a way that makes it utterly plain that we are not – quite – dealing with the real world. This perhaps explains too the luminous quality of the word ASPHALT as it is spelled out in glowing letters during the opening sequence.

14 For a late example of this city/countryside opposition, which appears to come down firmly in favour of loyalty and the countryside, see Murnau's first American film, *Sunrise: A Song of Two Humans*, which of course predates *Asphalt*. Note too, that although the vamp who seduces the husband is of course a city woman (city = excitement and danger), even going so far as to tempt the husband into leaving his loyal wife with the use of cinematic images of the city projected over the swamp, the couple's reconciliation likewise takes place during their trip to the city and a visit to an amusement park (city = excitement and opportunity). Indeed it is the storm on the lake (associated therefore with the country) which threatens to separate the newly-reconciled lovers for ever; see Fischer 1998.

15 Notice how Holk, once he is under the spell of Else's beauty, at times lumbers around like the somnambulist Cesare nearly a decade before.

16 As well as Dr Mabuse, the street is the home to Jack the Ripper

(Gustav Diessl in *Pandora's Box*), Mackie the Knife (Rudolf Forster in *The Threepenny Opera*) and the child murderer Beckert (Peter Lorre in *M*). Quoting Enno Patalas, Elsaesser discusses the three principal bogeymen in Weimar film as 'the witchmaster Dr Caligari, the vampire Nosferatu and the gambler Mabuse' (2000b: 190, n. 31; see also 2000b: 19f). The reality is that the films of this period are overflowing with such monsters and increasingly they are associated with the city in a love/hate symbiotic relationship.

FILMOGRAPHY

Abwege (*The Devious Path*) (G. W. Pabst, 1926, Germany)
Alraune (*A Daughter of Destiny*) (Henrik Galeen, 1928, Germany)
Der Andere (*The Other*) (Max Mack, 1913, Germany)
Der Andere (*The Other*) (Robert Wiene, 1930, Germany)
Anna Boleyn (Ernst Lubitsch, 1920, Germany)
Asphalt (Joe May, 1929, Germany)
Bronenosets Potyomkin (*Battleship Potemkin*) (Sergei Eisenstein, 1926, Soviet Union)
Berlin: Die Symphonie der Großstadt (*Berlin: Symphony of a Big City*) (Walter Ruttmann, 1927, Germany)
Birth of a Nation (D. W. Griffith, 1915, USA)
Blade af Satans bog (*Leaves from Satan's Book*) (Carl Theodor Dreyer, 1921, Denmark)
Blade Runner (Ridley Scott, 1982, USA)
Chelovek s kino-apparatom (*Man with a Movie Camera*) (Dziga Vertov, 1929, Soviet Union)
Der blaue Engel (*The Blue Angel*) (Josef von Sternberg, 1929, Germany)
Der blaue Junge (*The Blue Boy*) (F. W. Murnau, 1919)
Das Boot (*The Boat*) (Wolfgang Petersen, 1981, Germany)
Die Brücke (*The Bridge*) (Berhard Wicki, 1959, Germany)
Die Büchse der Pandora (*Pandora's Box*) (G. W. Pabst, 1929, Germany)
Das Cabinet des Dr Caligari (*The Cabinet of Dr Caligari*) (Robert Wiene, 1920, Germany)
Close Encounters of the Third Kind (Steven Spielberg, 1977, USA)
Dr Mabuse, der Spieler (*Dr Mabuse, The Gambler)* (Fritz Lang, 1922, Germany)
Die Dreigroschenoper (*The Threepenny Opera/The Beggar's Opera*) (G. W. Pabst, 1931, Germany)

Es geschah am 20. Juli (*It Happened on July 20th*) (G. W. Pabst, 1955, Germany)

Der ewige Jude (*The Eternal Jew*) (Fritz Hippler, 1940, Germany)

F.P.1 antwortet nicht (*F.P.1 Is Not Answering*) (Karl Hartl, 1933, Germany)

Die Fahrt nach Hamburg (Joe May, 1911, Germany)

Faust (F. W. Murnau, 1926, Germany)

Der Farmer aus Texas (*The Farmer from Texas*) (Joe May, 1925, Germany)

Frankenstein (James Whale, 1931, USA)

Die Frau im Mond (*The Woman in the Moon*) (Fritz Lang, 1929, Germany)

Die freudlose Gasse (*The Joyless Street*) (G. W. Pabst, 1925, Germany)

Fury (Fritz Lang, 1936, USA)

Die Gehimnisse einer Seele (*Secrets of a Soul*) (G. W. Pabst, 1926, Germany)

Die geheimnisvolle Villa (Joe May, 1914, Germany)

Genuine (Robert Wiene, 1920, Germany)

A Girl in Every Port (Howard Hawks, 1928, USA)

Der Golem (*The Golem*) (Henrik Galeen, 1915, USA)

Der Golem, wie er in die Welt kam (*The Golem: How He Came Into the World*) (Paul Wegener & Carl Boese, 1920, Germany)

Gräfin Donelli (G. W. Pabst, 1924, Germany)

La Grande illusion (*The Grand Illusion*) (Jean Renoir, 1937, France)

Greed (Erich von Stroheim, 1924, USA)

Halbblut (*The Half-Caste*) (Fritz Lang, 1919, Germany)

Hangmen Also Die (Fritz Lang, 1943, USA)

Heimkehr (*Homecoming*) (Joe May, 1925, Germany)

Herrin der Welt (*Mistress of the World*) (Joe May, 1919–20, Germany)

Homunculus (Otto Rippert, 1916, Germany)

Im Banne der Kralle (*Under the Spell of the Claw*) Carl Fröhlich, 1921, Austria)

Das indische Grabmal (*The Indian Today*) (Joe May, 1921, Germany)

INRI (*Crown of Thorns*) (Robert Wiene, 1923, Germany)

Die Insel der Seligen (Max Reinhardt, 1913, Germany)

The Invisible Man Returns (Joe May, 1940, USA)

It (Clarence Badger, 1927, USA)

Der Januskopf (*Dr. Jekyl and Mr. Hyde*) (F. W. Murnau, 1920, Germany)

Kameradschaft (*Comradeship*) (G. W. Pabst, 1931, Germany)

King Kong (Merian Cooper, 1933, USA)

Kuhle Wampe oder Wem gehört die Welt? (Slatan Dudow, 1932, Germany)

Der letzte Mann (*The Last Laugh)* (F. W. Murnau, 1925, Germany)

Die Liebe der Jeanne Ney (*The Love of Jeanne Ney*) (G. W. Pabst, 1927, Germany)

The Longest Day (Ken Annakin, Andrew Marton, Bernhard Wicki, Darryle F. Zanuck, 1962, USA)

M (Fritz Lang, 1931, Germany)

Madame Dubarry (*Passion*) (Ernst Lubitsch, 1919, Germany)

Menschen am Sonntag (*People on Sunday*) (Curt Siodmak, Robert Siodmak, Edgar G. Ulmer & Fred Zinnemann, 1930, Germany)

Metropolis (Fritz Lang, 1927, Germany)

Metoroporisu (*Metropolis*) (Osamu Tezuka, 2001, Japan)

Der müde Tod (*Between Two Worlds*) (Fritz Lang, 1921, Germany)

Music in the Air (Joe May, 1934, USA)

Die Nibelungen: Siegfried (*Siegfried's Death*) (Fritz Lang, 1924, Germany)

Die Nibelungen: Kriemhilds Rache (*Kriemhild's Revenge*) (Fritz Lang, 1924, Germany)

Nosferatu: eine Symphonie des Grauens (*Nosferatu: A Symphony of Horror*) (F. W. Murnau, 1922, Germany)

Nosferatu: Phantom der Nacht (Werner Herzog, 1979, Germany)

Orlacs Hände (*The Hands of Orlac*) (Robert Wiene, 1924, Germany)

Panik in Chicago (*Panic in Chicago*) (Robert Wiene, 1931, Germany)

Phantom (*The Phantom*) (F. W. Murnau, 1922, USA)

Raskolnikow (Robert Wiene, 1923, Germany)

Der Rosenkavalier (Robert Wiene, 1925, USA)

Satanas (*Satan*) (F. W. Murnau, 1919, Germany)

Scarlet Street (Fritz Lang, 1945, USA)

Der Schatz (*The Treasure*) (G. W. Pabst, 1923, USA)

Schloss Vogelöd (*The Haunted Castle*) (F. W. Murnau, 1921, Germany)

Shadow of the Vampire (E. Elias Merhige, 2000, USA)

Spinnen (*The Spide*) (Fritz Lang, 1919 & 1920, Germany)

Spione (*Spies*) (Fritz Lang, 1928, Germany)

Der Spuk im Haus des Professors (Joe May, 1914, Germany)

Die Straße (*The Street*) (Karl Grune, 1923, Germany)

Der Student von Prag (*The Student of Prague*) (Paul Wegener & Stellan Rye, 1913, Germany)

Sunrise: A Song of Two Humans (F. W. Murnau, 1927, USA)

Tabu (F. W. Murnau, 1930, USA)

Das Tagebuch einer Verlorenen (*The Diary of a Lost Woman*) (G. W. Pabst, 1929, Germany)

Taifun (Robert Wiene, 1933, Germany)

Das Todestelephon (Oskar Messter, 1912, Germany)

The Thief of Bagdad (Raoul Walsh, 1924, USA)

Torgus (Hanz Kobe, 1921, Germany)

Tragödie der Liebe (*Tragedy of Love*) (Joe May, 1922, Germany)
Triumph des Willens (*Triumph of the Will*) (Leni Riefenstahl, 1934, Germany)
Ultimatum (Robert Wiene, 1938, France)
Veritas Vincit (Joe May, 1919, Germany)
Le Voyage dans le lune (*A Trip to the Moon*) (Goerges Méliès, 1902, France)
Von Morgens bis Mitternachts (*From Morn to Midnight*) (Karl Heinz Martin, 1920, Germany)
Das Wachsfigurenkabinett (The *Waxworks*) (Paul Leni, 1924, Germany)
Das Weib des Pharao (Ernst Lubitsch, 1922, Germany)
Westfront 1918 (G. W. Pabst, 1930, Germany)
Wings (William A. Wellmann, 1927, USA)

BIBLIOGRAPHY

Altenloh, Emilie (2001 [1913]) 'A Sociology of the Cinema: the Audience', in
   Screen. 43, 3 (Autumn), 249–93.
Anz, Thomas and Michael Stark (eds) (1982) *Expressionismus: Manifeste und
   Dokumente zur deutschen Literatur 1910–1920*. Stuttgart: Metzler.
Atwell, Lee (1977) *G. W. Pabst*. Boston: Twayne.
Balázs, Béla (1970) *The Theory of the Film: Character and Growth of a New Art*.
   New York: Dover Publications.
Becker, Klaus and Gerd Albrecht (1981) *Friedrich Wilhelm Murnau: ein großer
   Regisseur der 20er Jahre*. Kassel: Stadtsparkasse Kassel.
Bordwell, David and Kristin Thompson (1994) *Film History: An Introduction*. New
   York: McGraw-Hill.
____ (2001) *Film Art: An Introduction* (6th edition). New York: McGraw-Hill.
Borgelt, Hans (1993) *Die Ufa – ein Traum*. Berlin: edition q.
Budd, Mike (ed.) (1990) *The Cabinet of Dr Caligari*. New Brunswick: Rutgers
   University Press.
Calhoon, Kenneth S. (ed.) (2001) *Peripheral Visions: The Hidden Stages of
   Weimar Cinema*. Detroit: Wayne State University Press.
Clarke, David (1997) *The Cinematic City*. London and New York: Routledge.
Coates, Paul (1991) *The Gorgon's Gaze: German Cinema, Expressionism, and the
   Legacy of Horror*. Cambridge: Cambridge University Press.
Cooke, Paul (2002) *German Expressionist Films*. Harpenden: Pocket Essentials.
Dalichow, Bärbel and Axel Geiss (1994) *Filmstadt Babelsberg*. Potsdam: Nicolai.
Deleuze, Gilles (1986) 'Montage', in *Cinema 1 – The Movement Image*.
   Minneapolis: University of Minnesota Press, 29–55.

Dube, Wolf-Dieter (1996 [1972]) *The Expressionists*. London: Thames and Hudson.

Edschmid, Kasimir (1961) *Expressionismus*. Munich, Vienna, Basle: Kurt Desch.

Eibel, Alfred (ed.) (1964) *Fritz Lang*. Paris: Présence du cinéma.

Eisner, Lotte (1969) *The Haunted Screen: Expressionism in the German Cinema and the Influence of Max Reinhardt*. London: Thames & Hudson.

_____ (1973) *Murnau*. London: Secker & Warburg.

_____ (1976) *Fritz Lang*. London: Secker & Warburg.

Elsaesser, Thomas (2000a) *Weimar Cinema and After: Germany's Historical Imaginary*. London and New York: Routledge.

_____ (2000b) *Metropolis*. London: British Film Institute.

Esser, Michael (ed.) (1994) *Gleißende Schatten: Kamerapioniere der zwanziger Jahre*. Berlin: Henschel Verlag.

Ezra, Elizabeth (ed.) (2004) *European Cinema*. Oxford: Oxford University Press.

Fischer, Lucy (1998) *Sunrise: A Song of Two Humans*. London: British Film Institute.

Fulbrook, Mary (1992) *A Concise History of Germany*. Cambridge: Cambridge University Press.

_____ (2002) *A History of Germany: The Divided Nation*. Oxford: Blackwell.

Garncarz, Josepeh (2004) 'Art and Industry: German Cinema of the 1920s', in Lee Grieveson and Peter Krämer (eds) *The Silent Cinema Reader*. London and New York: Routledge, 389–400.

Gunning, Tom (2000) *The Films of Fritz Lang: Allegories of Vision and Modernity*. London: British Film Institute.

Hake, Sabine (2002) *German National Cinema*. London and New York: Routledge.

Hofmannsthal, Hugo von (2004) 'The Substitute for Dreams', in Richard McCormick and Alison Guenther-Pal (eds) *German Essays on Film*. New York: Continuum, 52–6.

Huyssen, Andreas (1996) 'The Vamp and the Machine: Fritz Lang's *Metropolis*', in Terri Ginsberg and Kirsten Moana Thompson (eds) *Perspectives on German Cinema*. New York: Simon and Schuster/Macmillan, 624–40.

Jacobsen, Wolfgang, Anton Kaes and Hans Helmut Prinzler (eds) (1993) *Die Geschichte des deutschen Films*. Stuttgart/Weimar: Metzler.

Jameux, Charles (1965) *F. W. Murnau*. Paris: Classiques du Cinéma.

Jenkins, Stephen (ed.) (1981) *Fritz Lang: The Image and the Look*. London: British Film Institute.

Jung, Uli and Walter Schatzberg (1999) *Beyond Caligari: The Films of Robert Wiene*. New York and Oxford: Berghahn.

Kaes, Anton (1993) 'Film in der Weimarer Republik: Motor der Moderne', in Wolfgang Jacobsen, Anton Kaes and Hans Helmut Prinzler (eds) *Die Geschichte des deutschen Films*. Stuttgart/Weimar: Metzler, 39–100.

____ (2002) 'Siegfried – A German Film Star', in Tim Bergfelder, Erica Carter and Deniz Göktürk (eds) *The German Cinema Book*. London: British Film Institute, 63–70.

____ (2004) 'Weimar Cinema: The Predicament of Modernity', in Elizabeth Ezra (ed.) *European Cinema*. Oxford: Oxford University Press, 59–77.

Kessler, Frank and Eva Warth (2002) 'Early Cinema and its Audiences', in Tim Bergfelder, Erica Carter and Deniz Göktürk (eds) *The German Cinema Book*. London: British Film Institute, 121–8.

Kracauer, Siegfried (1947) *From Caligari to Hitler: A Psychological History of the German Film*. Princeton, NJ: Princeton University Press.

____ (1995a [1927]) 'The Mass Ornament', in Thomas Y. Levin (ed.) *Siegfried Kracauer: The Mass Ornament* (*Weimar Essays*). Cambridge, MA: Harvard University Press, 75–86.

____ (1995b [1926]) 'Calico World', in Thomas Y. Levin (ed.) *Siegfried Kracauer: The Mass Ornament* (*Weimar Essays*). Cambridge, MA: Harvard University Press, 281–90.

____ (1995c [1927]) 'The Little Shop Girls go to the Movies', in Thomas Y. Levin (ed.) *Siegfried Kracauer: The Mass Ornament* (*Weimar Essays*). Cambridge, MA: Harvard University Press, 291–304.

Kreimeier, Klaus (1999 [1992]) *The Ufa-Story: A History of Germany's Greatest Film Company 1918–1945*. Berkeley: University of California Press.

Kurtz, Rudolf (1965) *Expressionismus im Film*. Zurich: Diogenes.

Lang, Fritz (2004 [1924]) 'The Artistic Composition of the Film Drama', in Richard McCormick and Alison Guenther-Pal (eds) *German Essays on Film*. New York: Continuum, 60–6.

Levin, Thomas Y. (ed.) (1995) *Siegfried Kracauer: The Mass Ornament* (*Weimar Essays*). Cambridge, MA: Harvard University Press.

Manvell, Roger and Heinrich Fraenkel (1971) *The German Cinema*. London: J. M. Dent & Sons.

Marc, Franz (1982) 'Die "Wilden" Deutschlands. In *Der blaue Reiter* 1912', in Thomas Anz and Michael Stark (eds) *Expressionismus: Manifeste und Dokumente zur deutschen Literatur 1910–1920*. Stuttgart: Metzler, 27–8.

McCormick, Richard and Alison Guenther-Pal (eds) (2004) *German Essays on Film*. New York: Continuum.

McGilligan, Patrick (1997) *Fritz Lang: The Nature of the Beast*. London: Faber and Faber.

Metzger, Rainer (2007) *Berlin in the 1920s*. London: Thames and Hudson.

Minden, Michael (2000) 'Fritz Lang's *Metropolis* and the United States', *German Life and Letters*, 53, 3, 340–50.

Müller, Robert (1994) 'Lichtbildner: Zur Arbeit des Kameramannes', in Michael Esser (ed.) *Gleißende Schatten: Kamerapioniere der zwanziger Jahre*. Berlin: Henschel Verlag, 35–62.

Mulvey, Laura (1989) *Visual and Other Pleasures*. London: Macmillan.

Murnau, F. W. (2004 [1928]) 'The Ideal Picture Needs No Titles', in Richard McCormick and Alison Guenther-Pal (eds) *German Essays on Film*. New York: Continuum, 66–8.

Murphy, Richard J. (1991) 'Carnival Desire and the Sideshow of Fantasy: Dream, Duplicity and Representational Instability in *The Cabinet of Dr. Caligari*', *The Germanic Review,* 66, 1, 48–56.

Petro, Patrice (1989) *Joyless Streets: Women and Melodramatic Representation in Weimar Germany*. Princeton: Princeton University Press.

Pike, David L. (2004) '"Kaliko-Welt": The *Großstädte* of Lang's *Metropolis* and Brecht's *Dreigroschenoper*', *Modern Language Notes*, 119, 474–505.

Prawer, Siegfried (1980) *Caligari's Children: The Film as Tale of Terror*. Oxford: Oxford University Press.

____ (1995) *Das Cabinet des Dr. Caligari: Drehbuch von Carl Mayer und Hans Janowitz zu Robert Wienes Film 1919/1920*. Munich: edition text + kritik.

Prinzler, Hans Helmut (ed.) (2003) *Friedrich Wilhelm Murnau: ein Melancholiker des Films*. Berlin: Bertz.

Raabe, Paul (1974) 'What is Expressionism', in *The Era of Expressionism*. London: Calder and Boyers, 11–13.

Roberts, Graham and Heather Wallis (2002) *Key Film Texts*. London and New York: Arnold, 28–32.

Roberts, Ian (2004) 'Caligari revisited: circles, cycles and counter-revolution in Robert Wiene's *Das Cabinet des Dr. Caligari*', *German Life and Letters*, 57, 2, 175–87.

____ (2007) 'Friedrich Wilhelm Murnau, transatlantic thresholds and transcendental homelessness', *Studies in European Cinema*, 4, 3, 223–33.

Robinson, David (1973) *World Cinema: A Short History*. London: Methuen.

____ (1997) *Das Cabinet des Dr. Caligari*. London: British Film Institute.

Rotha, Paul (1967) *The Film Till Now: A Survey of World Cinema*. London: Spring Books.

Salt, Barry (1979) 'From *Caligari* to who?', *Sight and Sound*, 48, 2 (Spring), 119–23.

Sandford, John (1995) 'Chaos and Control in the Weimar Film', *German Life and Letters*, 48, 3, 311–23.

Scherber, Jürgen (1990) *Damals in Neubabelsberg: Studios, Stars und Kinopaläste*. Leipzig: Edition Leipzig.

Schlüpmann, Heide (1992) 'Early German Cinema: Melodrama – Social Drama', in Richard Dyer and Ginette Vincendeau (eds) *Popular European Cinema*. London and New York: Routledge, 206–19.

Shepard, Jim (1998) *Nosferatu in Love*. London: Faber & Faber.

Sinclair, Andrew (ed.) (1971) *G. W. Pabst: Pandora's Box (Lulu)*. London: Lorrimer Publishing.

Smedley, Nick (1993) 'Fritz Lang's trilogy: the rise and fall of a European social commentator', *Film History*, 5, 1, 1–21.

Ward, Janet (2001) *Weimar Surfaces: Urban Culture in 1920s Germany*. Berkeley: University of California Press.

INDEX

www.ingramcontent.com/pod-product-compliance
Ingram Content Group UK Ltd.
Pitfield, Milton Keynes, MK11 3LW, UK
UKHW032040230125
454070UK00004B/154